Dearest Joan & Steve,

May you be Blessed
with Eternal Inner Security
and Infinite Wealth.
                    Love,
                 Canista & Jared
                   5/03

DEAR JOAN + STEVE —
   I WISH YOU A LIFETIME
OF APPRECIATION AND ABUNDANCE

IN ALL FORMS
                    IN JOY —
                    Stu

"It's refreshing to encounter an enlightened perspective on the deeper meaning of security. True security is a treasure everyone wants, but few are able to attain. The insights and practical tools presented here will go a long ways to catalyzing self reliance, deep trust and true security."

Michael Toms, President of
New Dimensions World Broadcasting Network and
Author of *A Time For Choices: Deep Dialogues
for Deep Democracy.*

"Inner Security and Infinite Wealth is a spiritual and practical approach to the fulfillment of our own longing for security. The authors enable the reader to delve into one's own limitless inner resources, where wealth and security truly live. This is a wonderful and inspiring read and I highly recommend it."

Lynne Twist, Author, *The Soul of Money.*

"I believe the new model for achieving wealth and inner understanding found in this book is right on course. I support these principals and believe that they are a part of the greater vision for human kind. I recommend this book for helping in achieving financial success, emotional and spiritual freedom."

Dannion Brinkley, International Best Selling
Author of *Saved By The Light* and
Founder of Compassion in Action.

"If you are looking for the deeper meaning in life, *Inner Security and Infinite Wealth* sheds light on the subject. Enjoy!"

Marilyn Tam, Author of *How to Use What
You've Got to Get What You Want,*
former President of Reebok Apparel and
former CEO of Aveda Corporation.

"An extraordinary book…with an emotionally intelligent message."

Ayman Sawaf, Co-Author, *Executive EQ—Emotional Intelligence in Leadership and Organizations*

"Reading *Inner Security and Infinite Wealth* is an investment in yourself—with huge potential for appreciation."

Donald Bronstein, Managing Director, [Major Wall Street Brokerage Firm]

"Inner Security and Infinite Wealth provides a methodology for self-awareness to focus your resources to achieve optimal balance in life."

Jerry Weintraub, Managing General Partner, Weintraub Capital Management, LLC

"Inner Security and Infinite Wealth reminds us that true wealth beyond measure resides only within us."

Pete Keeler, CEO, Arrive Technologies, Inc.

"This book is a tool to stop, look inside, discover what is possible and then find peace."

Randy Kauffman, President, Next Energy Corp.

"An excellent example of a financial primer for the new millenium, in every sense. Its open and encouraging tone makes it an invaluable tool for those seeking true financial security and independence."

Dave Rogen, President, Rogen Consulting

INNER SECURITY & INFINITE WEALTH

Merging Self Worth and Net Worth

STUART ZIMMERMAN & JARED ROSEN

SelectBooks, Inc.

Inner Security & Infinite Wealth:
Merging Self Worth and Net Worth
©2003 by Stuart Zimmerman and Jared Rosen

DreamSculpt Publishing produces books and media that inspire a world
in which creativity; integrity, love and wisdom are the cornerstones.

This edition published by SelectBooks, Inc.
For information, address SelectBooks, Inc., New York, New York.

ISBN 1-59079-055-3

Library of Congress Cataloging-in-Publication Data

Zimmerman, Stuart, 1957–
  Inner security & infinite wealth : merging self worth and net worth /
Stuart Zimmerman, Jared Rosen.
  p. cm.
ISBN 1-59079-055-3 (hardbound)
  1. Money–Philosophy.
  2. Wealth–Moral and ethical aspects.
  3. Security (Psychology)
  4. Quality of life.
  5. Investments–Moral and ethical aspects.
  I. Title: Inner security and infinite wealth.
  II. Rosen, Jared, 1955–
III. Title.
HG220.3.Z56 2003
332.024'01–dc21

                    2003004848

Manufactured in the United States of America

10 9 8 7 6 5 4 3 2 1

To Teri, with Eternal Love and Gratitude

ACKNOWLEDGMENTS

To Carista Luminare-Rosen: We deeply appreciate your unwavering dedication and constant support throughout the writing of this book. Your uncompromising standard for excellence has taken the substance of this book to another level.

To Hollin Zimmerman: We express heartfelt gratitude for leading us deeper into our truth and for providing a loving atmosphere for creativity to flow.

To all of our children: Kylea, Ilana, Genevieve, Nathan, Kai and Sofia—you are our teachers of unconditional love and the inspiration for dedicating our lives to creating a safer, more loving world.

To our parents: Thank you for encouraging us to pursue happiness in our lives.

To Kenzi Sugihara: We express our gratitude for your patience, wit and practical guidance on this project.

To Pam Gentry: Thank you for joining our team and playing together in so many ways. Your positive energy and good taste are always welcome.

Thanks to our editors—Dana Isaacson and Todd Barmann for your craftsmanship and dedication to excellence.

Thank you Kathleen Isaksen for your artistic vision and patience.

Thank you Maryglenn McCombs for showing up just in time and offering your practical approach to publicity.

Thank you Bill Gladstone for galvanizing the team.

Additional thanks to: Jerry Weintraub. Pete Keeler, David Solomon, Dan Blumberg, Bob Pryt, Ranjita Ryan, Leianna Hollingsworth, Mark and Clint Gelotte, Stuart Rudick, Ayman Sawaf, Gary Shemano, Michael Klein, Michael Gosney, Danny Murphy, Lee Twomey and Mary Cosgrove for your support, encouragement and friendship.

INNER
SECURITY
&
INFINITE
WEALTH

CONTENTS

Eight Treasures of Inner Security
and Infinite Wealth

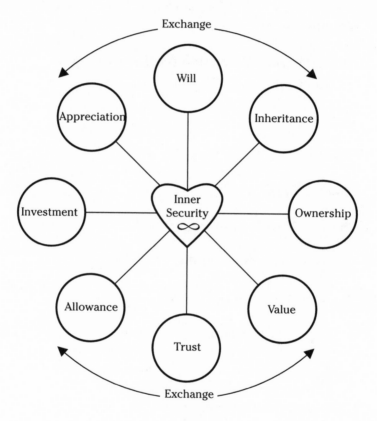

INTRODUCTION—
EIGHT TREASURES OF
INNER SECURITY AND INFINITE WEALTH

What follows are dialogues between the two authors over the span of one year. Through these conversations, they transform eight everyday financial terms into practical tools for life mastery. As true wealth and security are created from the inside out, each one of these terms has an application in both the inner and the outer worlds.

Illustrated on the opposite page are the "Eight Treasures of Inner Security and Infinite Wealth." Inner Security, the heart of all the treasures, is a limitless state of inner peace, richness and fulfillment.

TREASURE ONE: **Will**—In the outer world, a will is a legal document in which you declare your final set of wishes for the disposition of your property. The inner will is the creative life force with which you achieve your heart's deepest desires.

TREASURE TWO: **Inheritance**—An inheritance is a set of tangible and intangible items you receive from an ancestor or predecessor. In its broadest sense, your inheritance is every thought, belief and action that has ever existed.

TREASURE THREE: **Ownership**—Ownership is most commonly associated with having and controlling property. Going deeper into this concept, you can take ownership of your self-identity and consciously shape it to support the manifestation of your dreams.

TREASURE FOUR: **Value**—Value is a measure of monetary worth. Through the embodiment and implementation of virtues and ideals, you increase self-worth and give your life greater meaning and value.

TREASURE FIVE: **Trust**—A trust is a legal entity designed for the safekeeping of valuables for the benefit of another. With trust in your values, you have the self-confidence from which to manifest your heart's desires.

TREASURE SIX: **Allowance**—An allowance is commonly an amount of money given on a regular basis. Funded by trust, allowance is also the permission you give yourself to take an action step in the direction of your dreams.

TREASURE SEVEN: **Investment**—An investment is an outlay of money for income or profit. Investment is also a longer-term expression of trust, committing all of your personal resources—including time, energy and money—toward the actualization of your dreams.

TREASURE EIGHT: **Appreciation**—Appreciation is the increase of value of your investment or property. With gratitude, each moment of your life takes on greater richness.

Through these "Eight Treasures," you can establish an enlightened state of Inner Security as well as a greater sense of financial security. Through Exchange, you share your sense of Inner Security with others. You also get to exchange the dreams you have attained for even greater ones. You can truly create infinite wealth from the inside out. There are no limits!

Throughout the book, one author, "the visionary," questions the other author, "the achiever." The responses are primarily global in nature, and exemplified by accounts of the achiever's personal life experience. Together, both authors question you. Your answers may change over time. They hold the key to your relationship to money and to yourself.

PROLOGUE

A conversation on the evening of September 10, 2001

September 10, 2001—What a blessing life is! It is always a joy to spend time with people who appreciate life as much as you do. With the setting sun revealing a magenta sky, two men enjoyed the simple luxury of a stimulating conversation as they walked along the beach. They spoke about their life, their family and their dreams. They discovered they had a mutual, burning desire to create Paradise on Earth for themselves, their children and for everyone else. That was their bond.

One man, an "achiever in life," had just stepped away from his multi-million dollar money management firm to discover security beyond the securities industry. The other man, a "visionary thinker," had dedicated his life work to create a world in which love is the highest standard, for education, for business, for all facets of life.

Admiring the timeless beauty of twilight, they each expressed how incredible life is, and can be. The invigorating energy of the rolling surf and salt air served to support and confirm their observation. The visionary intuited our time and place in history. He spoke about how greed, insensitivity and, at times, intentional deception had created an atmosphere of heartlessness in the world of finance. He spoke of how this new millennium is an opportunity to change the course of history. He challenged his friend, the achiever, to set a course of action to manifest their mutual dream—a world of peace and harmony where love, compassion and money flow together seamlessly.

The achiever beamed like a beacon through the emerging coastal fog. With great passion he screamed into the night air, "I feel great! I feel incredible!" He then paused with a deep breath to savor the moment as he spoke in a soft yet firm voice, "Right here, right now, this moment is perfect exactly the way it is." With a smile from ear to ear he proclaimed, "This moment has never existed before...

"Anything is possible!"

September 11, 2001—The unthinkable occurs. An act of terrorism takes the lives of thousands of innocent people on our own soil. The World Trade Center—the heart of global finance... razed to the ground. Zero.

CAPITALISM HAS A HEART ATTACK!

In the midst of such horror, through the ash and dust, it was clear...

There is more to security than money and matter.

Everything we have in the material world can be taken from us in a heartbeat.

True security, inner security, cannot.

The events of 9-11 have blown the doors of possibility wide open for all of us. How we respond to these uncertain times will determine our future, individually and collectively. We can act and react with mistrust. Each of us can identify with the anxiety associated with more potential terrorism or the seeming loss of opportunities for financial growth and freedom. In a state of fear, we can easily create a world dominated by struggle, increased violence and continued economic contraction. This may be one realistic scenario—one of many possibilities.

There is a flip side to this coin. Because anything is possible, even our grandest dreams and ideals are attainable. Each of us has the freedom and the power to love each other and our self without limit. Each of us has the capability to modify or re-invent our self-identity so that we can achieve our individual goals in this lifetime. Collectively, we can re-direct our substantial aggregate resources, including vast sums of money, into areas that create health, peace and prosperity.

An Invitation

We cordially invite you to experience
Inner Security and Infinite Wealth.

Please come as you are.

Bring your willingness to feel your heart's desires…

To fulfill your grandest dreams.

For this moment has never existed before…

Are you ready to discover that…

anything is possible!

Inner Security

The real treasure is inside.

Only you can open the door.

Inner Security

*It was a bright, sunny day as the visionary and achiever took a walk in the hills only days after the horrors of 9-11. As they paused in a peaceful meadow, they noticed how still the air was. Birds floated among the trees and soared above in their daily rituals. With the airports shut down, the stock market in suspended animation and the country gripped in terror, the two men closed their eyes to share a moment of silence—to experience the moment and **feel** the silence.*

The last moment has just passed away.

All you have now is *this* moment.

All that you think you have...

All that you think you need...

All that you think you want...

All can vanish in a heartbeat.

In this moment, what security do you have?

Homeland security?

Social Security?

Financial security?

To many, financial security is the mother of all securities. Security can be defined as freedom from worry. Financial security is the quest to eliminate worries about money. This is why financial security (the mother of all securities) has given birth to an entire industry: the securities industry.

SECURITY EQUALS FREEDOM FROM WORRY.

The securities industry was specifically designed to foster shared prosperity. And yet, for so many people financial security remains either elusive or simply a dream. And still, for many of those who have amassed much wealth, financial security has often not resulted in freedom from worry.

What kind of security is that?

Clearly, having money does not equate freedom from worry. However, there is also no denying that your relationship to money is a significant component of a greater sense of security.

How many people really feel secure about money? Who among us hasn't spent hours worrying about money matters? How many people spend hours a day dealing with others in conflict around issues associated with money? Think about all of the fights with spouses, divorce settlements and failed business relationships, all centered on the theme of money and security.

Why has money been the basis of so much pain and conflict?

One answer to this question is because people feel betrayed.

Betrayed by money.

Betrayed by another.

Betrayed by a belief...

Or a lack of something to believe in.

How can we trust in money with such a legacy of betrayal?

Perhaps the most pertinent question is, "Can we trust in money without trusting in ourselves first?" Can we trust the people with whom we are in financial relationships?

It is hard to trust in money when it feels contaminated by greed, violence, infidelity, jealousy and countless forms of abuse.

Some people are so accustomed to a culture of mistrust that they feel like they can't trust anybody—including themselves.

Money has been the source of so much pain; everything that has meaning to us can be a source of pain. Loss and lack cause pain. Lost love can hurt deeply. The death of a loved one can leave us in despair. And the pain we feel can be just as much physical as it is emotional.

Good news: because you can feel so much pain, it means you can also feel the whole spectrum of emotions deeply. If you did not feel so deeply, your perception of loss or lack would not be so severe.

You have the capacity to experience limitless joy and creative power. All of this and more are within you. This is your inner security!

Inner security is freedom. Inner security is your right. The same kind of freedom and right envisioned by our forefathers and supported by the U. S. Constitution and proclaimed in the Declaration of Independence.

You have freedom of speech, of press, of assembly, of religion, of expression. You have the right to the pursuit of happiness. With inner security, you can apply these freedoms and rights to your life experience and create real inner wealth.

The freedom to think for yourself—

The freedom to speak what you feel—

The freedom to feel and experience as much as you possibly can—

The freedom to love beyond all pain and suffering—

The freedom to love beyond judgment—

The freedom from being bound by the past—

The freedom from worry about the future—

With inner security, you are free to give even more of who you are because you have more of yourself to give. You are open to receive even more than you ever have received before.

Including money!

Inner security is a rich state of being that offers infinite wealth. It is a sense of comfort and luxury independent of the outer circumstances and environment. This internal comfort flows from knowing that your life is based in love, compassion and gratitude. This foundation of love is the source of your actions. With inner security, you have nothing to prove to yourself or to others. And you have nothing to defend. You know you are doing your best...and with love.

WITH INNER SECURITY, YOU HAVE NOTHING TO REGRET, WORRY ABOUT OR JUDGE.

When your actions are not based on higher values, you encounter resistance in the world and, possibly, inner conflict as well. If struggle is not the path of preference, you can choose to return to your love-based foundation. You can return to your state of inner security. Living a life of inner security, you consistently free yourself from worry, regret and judgment. Eventually it becomes both logical and second nature to you. A life of inner security is your natural and preferred state of being.

With inner security, you discover that you are a treasure— exactly the way you are. Once you have uncovered the infinite wealth that has always been inside you, you can share it with the world. As you unlock your treasure from within, you can project your fortune into the outer world. The outer world can then reflect it back to you.

With inner security, you can enjoy infinite wealth, a combination of both inner and outer wealth. The inner wealth you can experience is immeasurable. Your capacity to feel love, inner peace, joy and wholeness is endless. Therefore, there are no limits to how much pleasure you can receive from your outer wealth or material possessions. There are even no limits to how much money you can generate.

It all begins with your will.

Do you want to feel more secure?

What would make you feel more secure right now?

Can anything outside of yourself make you feel more secure?

Will

Ignite your will to fan the flames

of your deepest desires.

CHAPTER TWO

Will

It was a crisp fall day as the visionary and the achiever hiked up the mountain. A gust of wind blew through the trees as the leaves fell like stock prices. The visionary took a deep breath as he climbed up the rock ledge, and asked his favorite question: "So, how do we build Heaven on Earth?" The achiever gazed up at the mountain peak and replied: "Begin by creating the life you want for yourself. When you really engage your will, you can move mountains." The achiever broke into a grin as he continued: "And guess what? Your life need not end for your will to go into effect now."

What is your **Will?**

Your will is the reservoir of your wants and wishes, dreams and desires.

Everything you have ever wanted...

> Or could want...

> > Lives in your will.

All the decisions you have made...

> All the actions you have taken...

> > All the things you own, up to this very moment, *are* the product of your will and the will of others.

Your will is enormous!

Think about it.

Consider how your will has impacted the course of your life... so far.

And that merely covers the past!

Your will *is* enormous (even if you believe it's God's Will).

Feel the depth of this reservoir of your wants and wishes.

Feel the magnitude of your will, its intensity.

Your will is enormous (even if you may not feel it in this moment).

It is yours and yours alone.

Nobody can take it away from you.

Your will is free.

So you are completely free to want…

…whatever you want, whenever you
want it.

Including this very instant.

You are completely free to love…

and love what you want.

Right now…

In this breath that you take, ask yourself: "What do I really want? What do I really love?"

Do you want to love your self more deeply?

Do you want to fire the self-critic—the judge within?

Do you want to deport the saboteur that undermines your success through feelings of unworthiness?

Do you want your outer life to be a reflection of how deeply you love?

Do you want peace of mind?

When what you love is what you want, and what you want is what you love, your will and heart are one. You become a magnet. The people and resources you need to manifest your dreams are drawn to you. You forge a path of least resistance.

When your will and heart are divided, you experience inner conflict. You become less certain of how to achieve your goals. You are subject to increased doubt and judgment. This creates resistance. Resistance from within will draw resistance from the world around you.

For example, if an entrepreneur is trying to raise money for a business endeavor, yet his heart is not in it, he will be putting out mixed signals to potential investors. Well-spoken words and a convincing business plan can be diminished by a lack of authenticity. Whether they consciously know it or not, people feel it when your heart is not fully present. Conversely, when you are aligned and present on all levels, you discover how miraculously the universe supports your desire.

Your heart knows what you want. Learn to trust it. It may take some time before you really can trust your heart. And that's okay. Your dreams and heart's desires are worth it.

WHEN WHAT YOU LOVE IS WHAT YOU WANT, AND WHAT YOU WANT IS WHAT YOU LOVE, YOUR WILL AND HEART ARE ONE.

Sometimes people want things that they don't necessarily love. They want things that they need—sometimes they need them for their very survival. Do we really have to love everything that we need?

If we love our existence, then we can love the things we need to support and maintain our lives. For example, a person may need surgery, yet they may have an aversion to it. If they want the surgery because they love their body, or because they want to be healthy for their loved ones, then they still want what they love.

Think about one thing you really want. Hold the thought or image clearly in your mind. Feel this desire deeply … in your heart, in your belly, throughout your entire body. If you *will*.

Your will can be gentle and loving like a warm embrace.

It can be fixed and determined—as an *iron will*.

At times, your will can seem inaccessible, buried beneath your fears and pain.

At times, it feels that your will alone is not enough, that events beyond your control cannot be changed.

At times, you may even question your very will to live.

WHEN YOUR WILL AND HEART ARE DIVIDED, YOU EXPERIENCE INNER CONFLICT.

For example, a parent may experience the death of their child. No matter how great their will was to save or heal their son or daughter, they were unable to avert this heartbreaking tragedy.

Can you imagine if you lost your child? The child you brought into this world—the child you cuddled, nurtured and protected at all hours of day and night? The loss is unspeakable. Beyond words. The pain might be excruciating. The grief might be unbearable. A parent who loses a child may feel that life is not worth living. At some point, they will arrive at a crossroad; there, they can choose to believe life is too painful to live, or they can summon their will to live with the spirit of their beloved alive within them.

Your will cannot be taken away by anyone. It is always there at your beck and call.

When you feel life is unfair and you feel you have been cheated, this is an opportunity to go deeper into your will. To overcome loss or to ease pain, you can always ask yourself, "What do I want to experience right now?" You can find love, joy or gratitude in any moment and remember the reality that you are far greater than your life circumstances.

Why?

Because you have dreams.

> Some have come true.
> Some have been exceeded.
> Some have yet to be lived.

What does it take for my dreams to come true?

Your willingness to take action. Your will is the fuel. Your willingness is the ignition to actualize dreams. The deeper your desire, the greater your will, the stronger your will power to live the life you want.

Through your will, you create your life from the inside out. When you focus your mind on an intended outcome, you are merging will and mind. When you open your mind to infinite possibilities, your detachment offers greater opportunity for your will's creative energy to manifest itself.

If your intent is to have a successful career, first identify this to yourself precisely. Declare it in a mind cleared of resistance and doubt. As you do so, observe the intent set in your mind, feel the desire in your heart. Feel how much you love the thought and feeling of a fulfilling vocation. Now, you fuel your intent and your heart's desire through the dedication and work it takes to achieve this goal.

INTENT IS THE CREATIVE IMPULSE THAT CATALYZES WHAT YOU WANT.

LOVE IS THE ENERGY THAT MAGNETIZES WHAT YOU WANT.

WILL IS THE FUEL THAT MOBILIZES WHAT YOU WANT.

You are exercising your will.

What does exercising your will have to do with executing your will?

Executing your will refers to the legal will that goes into effect upon your death. Your will is a legal document in which you declare to whom your possessions are to go after your life has ended. This document is called the "Last Will and Testament" because it is designed to contain the final set of wishes for your property, revoking and superseding all prior instructions. And, you may revise your will to reflect changes in your desires.

Your last will and testament is important. Consider how much time, energy and dedication has been required of you in the pursuit of possessions. This is more than a legal document. Your will leaves a footprint of your lifetime that impacts generations to come. It may change the lives of your beneficiaries (and those you exclude) forever.

Your last will and testament is your final statement of wishes: the result of a lifetime of decisions and actions. Your last will and testament is not confined to distributing your tangible and financial assets. This is *your* final declaration of wishes. You can include your strongest desires for the lives of your loved ones as well: to let them know how much they mean to you, how much they enrich your life, how their will has affected yours.

I see how my last will and testament relates to inner will. How can I get my inner will in order?

Start by identifying your wishes. Then sort them in order of preference. By prioritizing that which has the most meaning in your life, you achieve greater clarity and energy to materialize your desires. This is especially helpful if you have conflicting or competing desires.

WITH YOUR WILL IN ORDER, YOU KNOW WHAT YOU WANT AND WHAT TO DO TO GET IT.

At times, my wants do conflict. Sometimes, two deep desires may be mutually exclusive. Let's say I want to

do what I love and I want to make a ton of money. What do I do in this case?

If there is a conflict, you need to delve deeply into your heart and identify what you want most. Prioritize. Perhaps you can be so passionate and effective in doing what you love that you can find a creative way to make your efforts lucrative as well. However, if there is a conflict between two wants that you cannot simultaneously fulfill, you need to choose between the two based on what you love the most. Your specific action steps will be determined by following the path of least resistance.

What do you say to the person who is in survival mode and feels like they don't even have the luxury to contemplate their true desires?

Each of us feels, at times, that we are in our own form of survival mode. It may be related to money issues, it may be related to caring for a loved one who is ill, it may be related to our own health. In those moments, dreams and heart's desires seem so distant. And still, even in times of despair, we have so much to be grateful for. With gratitude, we find our way back into our heart and what means most to us. Once we are present in our heart, we can access our true desires and follow the path of least resistance.

•   •   •

How in your life have you been able to follow the path of least resistance?

As a child, I loved sports and wanted to be a professional athlete. I also wanted to make a lot of money. When it came time to choose a career path I chose the path of money, because my desire to make money was very strong. By going to business school, I felt I was on a path of least resistance compared to my sense of what the path to becoming a professional athlete would be. I was also able to make this decision based on feeling what it was about sports that I loved and allowing myself to experience it through a career in the stock market. I had found an environment that presented me with the attributes of competitive sports.

I discovered I could get immediate feedback for my efforts in the stock market—just like in a sporting event. I was able to compete with some of the brightest minds in the world. Through the stock market, I experienced both the thrill of victory and the agony of defeat. I was able to reconcile my deepest desires and strongest intent. My heart and mind were in alignment.

Because my burning desire to manage my own firm was clear and strong, I was dedicated to waking up at four a.m. for fifteen years. I was devoted to pour my blood, sweat and tears into the success of this quest, and after fifteen years I achieved my dream. I exercised my will in harmony with intent and desire.

So why did you give up a career that was so thrilling and fulfilling?

Another deep desire became more important. Even if you have your will in order, you can always revise it. After almost twenty years of focusing on making money, the circumstances of my life required me to revise how I was applying my inner will.

On a Friday the 13th in November 1998 my partner was diagnosed with cancer in her bones. In short order, my whole world changed: I felt completely alone. Her first regimen of chemotherapy was so toxic to her system that she was bedridden.

I witnessed pain. Hers.

I felt pain. Mine.

Unlike anything I had ever experienced. I was completely powerless to heal her.

Powerlessness pervaded my being. I became increasingly sensitive when the market went against me, when I had difficulty making money. I *had* to make money. Every day. I needed to find worth as a human being through making money. I had to find some redeeming value. Something measurable. It's not like I could heal my dear friend.

So there I was, driving myself to make money every day, which in the stock market is unrealistic. I became enslaved. I grew angry. There I was, setting a ridiculously unattainable goal for myself, feeling lousy about not achieving it. And there was my partner in her bed, praying for her life.

How could I possibly allow making money to be such a high priority when my partner was fighting for her life?

How could I allow moneymaking to be such a high priority?

How could I possibly allow my net worth to determine my self worth?

How could I not?

I needed answers. I went deep into my will and into my heart's desires to start the process. My intent, desire and will to find these answers were in alignment. I began to discover some answers. I was clear in what was becoming most important to me. In doing so, I revised my will ... and my career path, accordingly.

Sometimes you need to revise your will because your actions do not feel consistent with your dreams. Sometimes you may need to ask if you are being true to yourself to please someone you love.

How much joy does it give you to please someone you love?

Are you creating more love for yourself and between the both of you in so doing?

How much do you deny your true nature in this process?

These are questions to ask yourself. Your heart will provide the answer. At any given moment, your answer may differ from past responses. This is what revising your will is about.

Every moment is a new moment.

In every moment, you are free to change your will to reflect changes in your desires.

Is it through my will that I make the choices in my life or is it the will of someone else being imposed on me?

Imposed will is a reality in which we all have experience. Just think about it. So many rules and regulations have been imposed on you from parents, teachers, government and society in general. So many actions and reactions of others have been imposed on you.

For me, as a child, imposed will shattered trust. When I had to sit in a twelve-by-twelve fluorescent-lit room and learn about algebraic equations, my will to learn seemed undermined. I felt powerless in the process of my education. My ability to choose what I wanted to learn and how I could learn was beyond my control. I am sure others have had similar experiences. How do we break this grip of imposed will?

Begin with yourself.

When your heart and will are one, you listen to and follow your heart's desire. You support others in following their own dreams and wishes rather than imposing your will on them. Further, you naturally minimize or eliminate drama when someone else seeks to impose will on you.

IN EVERY MOMENT, YOU ARE FREE
TO REVISE YOUR WILL TO REFLECT
CHANGES IN YOUR DESIRES.

Each one of your choices has consequences. This is why it is so important for you to align your intent and your will with your heart's desire. With love as your highest standard, you choose a life path of richness that enhances your prospects for peace and harmony. You have no desire to impose your will on others. You respect each individual's sovereignty as you promote your own.

You seem to be really passionate about your will. How do you gain clarity in knowing what you want?

Approach your inner will with the same focus and detail as your last will and testament. I actually list in order of importance what means the most to me. At times, the order of my desires changes, and that is the beauty of being able to revise it in the moment.

• • •

My Will

My will is:

To embody joy to its fullest.

To share this joy with others.

To provide an environment for others to experience their deepest heart's desires.

My will is:

To love my Creator more fully with each passing day.

To love myself as I love my Creator.

To love others as I love myself.

My will is:

To live in the present moment, free from past limitations, open to future possibilities.

To live a life at work, play, home and prayer without separation or distinction, so that it is all one state of being.

To create an external environment that reflects my sense of inner joy and abundance.

My will is:

To be a loving, caring and responsible father and husband.

To teach and remind my children how to love themselves more fully.

To extend family beyond bloodlines.

My will is:

To enjoy and honor my physical well-being.

To expand the capabilities of all my senses.

To respect the limitations of my physical body.

My will is:

To have total financial freedom.

To help redirect the flow of money into areas which create and promote love.

To attract others to join me in this endeavor.

My will is:

> To discover new and different ways in which to communicate love.

> To experience intimacy more deeply.

> To choose love over fear, judgment and greed.

My will is:

> To live a life of Inner Security.

> To create Heaven on Earth during my lifetime.

> To leave a blueprint for its sustainability for all who survive me.

Your expression of your will seems to be universal. We all want our desires fulfilled. Frequently, this requires money. How can people who do not have financial wealth experience the 'best' in their lives?

It is all in the eye of the beholder. Whatever you love, whatever you value, whatever you appreciate. What is the 'best' for you? Eating food that you grew in your own garden? Going to the most exclusive restaurant? Connecting with people you love? Feeling rich on the inside, or limiting your wealth to money? Feeling radiant and secure, or worried and fearful? Feeling free, or feeling stuck?

Even if you do not have financial wealth in this moment, you are free to choose to focus your desire on money...or not. Money becomes less of a struggle for you because you already feel rich, and that is what you want. When you do not have inner security, your choices are limited to external definition.

Each of you has the limitless capacity to love and to create. Your will is the first asset of infinite wealth.

For those who do have significant financial wealth, what is the 'best' for you? What do you want that you do not have right now? What dreams do you have that are still unfulfilled? What do you want to create with your resources?

You have achieved your net worth through exercising your will or by someone else exercising their will on your behalf. You have free rein to exercise your will again right now, to create what you want for your life, the lives of those you love and the world you love, right now.

You are free!

What is your will?

What legacy do you want to leave?

If your next breath was your last,
what legacy would you
leave today?

What is your will…
right now?

Inheritance

All the world is your inheritance.

Inheritance

The day after Thanksgiving was a perfect day for the visionary and achiever to get together for their weekly walk. The air was invigorating, especially considering how stuffed they were from the previous day of traditional overeating.

As they walked down the forest path, the visionary seemed to have some undigested feelings about the questions of the will. He asked the achiever, "If I can have everything I want, wouldn't it be too good to be true?" The achiever replied, "You know what comes after the will...the inheritance."

What is your inheritance?

The world is your inheritance. It is the product of all the wills of everyone who has ever lived.

All of the wonders and woes...

all of the possibilities of beauty, joy, creativity and infinite wealth;

all of the possibilities of fear, abuse, greed and destruction;

all of the beliefs of what life is and

all of the beliefs of what can and cannot be...

all are available to you...in every moment.

That's a vast inheritance! So, are you saying that we inherit more than the keepsakes of our parents?

Your parents *are* your inheritance ...

and all that they believe in.

Their beliefs about life and death;

their beliefs about God,

their beliefs about money;

their beliefs about themselves

and their beliefs about you.

You have inherited from your entire lineage.

Your body is your inheritance—

right down to your DNA.

You have inherited the genetic characteristics of your ancestors.

You have inherited the pain and struggle of your family history.

You have inherited the primal instinct to survive.

You have inherited the will to live.

You have inherited a sense of security...

And a sense of insecurity.

Your parents and their parents most likely inherited and directly experienced significant struggle and insecurity. They may have endured great hardships such as wartime, the Great Depression, poor working conditions and endless hours resulting in shorter, harder lives. No wonder the belief that 'life is hard' was so prevalent for prior generations. By our standards of today, it was. They may have concluded that there are more important things in life than love.

The conditions and experiences of your parents' lives shaped their will. At times, their choices may have been based more in fear than in love—due to insecurity. Their inherited beliefs may have felt like a ball and chain weighing them down. This burden may still exist today.

More than likely, they inherited the belief that money equals security. This may have motivated them to work hard to provide for you, so that your life would be easier than theirs.

MANY OF US INHERITED THE BELIEF THAT MONEY EQUALS SECURITY.

In addition to the beliefs you inherited directly from your lineage, you have inherited large-scale beliefs generated by society.

Many of these beliefs are fear-based. For generations, civilizations have struggled for survival or for conquest. This struggle is passed on through the memories of wars, discrimination, famine and scarcity in many forms. In turn, this sense of scarcity has generated its own legacy of insecurity.

Struggle and insecurity existed even for kings and queens. Many of those in power struggled to maintain and defend all that they had. This included the economic elite as well, for their insecurity translated into both fear of financial loss and fear of powerlessness as well as a mistaken belief equating self-worth with net worth.

This sounds like greed. Is that what you are referring to?

Greed is an exaggerated fear of loss that results in selfish desire beyond reason. A person of greed has an insatiable appetite. They seek to impose their will on others to feed their hunger for self worth. They believe economic power is the source of their life meaning.

In reality, they are dominated by fear and self-judgment. Their actions are not based in love.

GREED IS THE ANTITHESIS OF INNER SECURITY AND RESULTS IN SELFISH DESIRE BEYOND REASON.

Greed is a belief system that money is more important than love. That true inner security cannot be achieved. That money is the next best thing. That money is the most important scorecard of life. That wealth is finite. Greed can become a logical conclusion from this line of reason.

Greed is the antithesis of inner security, because it seeks to create wealth from the outside in, regardless of its impact on others. Whereas greed is based in fear and lack, inner security is based in love and limitless capacity. Greed does not allow for contentment in the moment. It does not allow for inner security in the moment.

Inner security is being free from inhibiting past beliefs.

If it is your will to achieve financial freedom, you may find that your beliefs about money may not fully support this quest. Consider the following prevailing attitudes and beliefs concerning money. Such as:

Money is the root of all evil.

Money makes the world go round.

Money can't buy you love.

Money talks.

Money = Stress.

Money doesn't grow on trees.

It takes money to make money.

I would rather be poor and happy than rich and miserable.

You can never be too rich or too thin.

You can marry more money in a minute than you can make in a lifetime.

If you marry for money, you end up earning it.

You get what you pay for.

Show me the money!

It's too good to be true.

Is it? Or can it be even better than you have imagined?

Your inheritance is limitless! Your inheritance is another asset of infinite wealth.

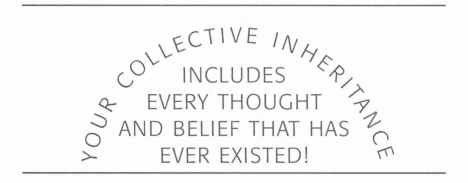

YOUR COLLECTIVE INHERITANCE INCLUDES EVERY THOUGHT AND BELIEF THAT HAS EVER EXISTED!

You have inherited the timeless quest for meaning and spiritual truth, the passion to search deeply for the inner light. It is up to you to summon your will and fuel this spark. It is up to you to accept and claim your divine inheritance.

What do you mean by claiming my "divine inheritance"?

Your divine inheritance is the total 'abundance of life' that is available to everyone equally. It is an inherent spiritual energy that offers all of us the potential to keep growing and evolving into the realization of our Essential Nature. This is sometimes referred to as the 'divine self' or 'higher self'. Your divine inheritance is anything you consider sacred and life giving, ranging from the most basic aspects of survival to the most sublime states of being—such as boundless joy or a life of miracles.

Considering all that is available to you, what are your deepest desires for your life, right now?

Review your beliefs, thoughts and patterns of behavior that separate the person you are now from who you want to be. In this moment, anything is possible. You can exchange anything and everything you took on from your parents that no longer serves you for the assets and values that enhance your life.

YOU HAVE INHERITED THE TIMELESS QUEST FOR MEANING AND SPIRITUAL TRUTH. CLAIM YOUR DIVINE INHERITANCE...NOW!

Clearly, your inheritance contains assets as well as liabilities. This is true for an actual monetary inheritance as well. It can be a great asset to you to inherit money after your parents pass. And it may be helpful to ask yourself probing questions to gain greater clarity such as: Does your quest for spiritual truth conflict with receiving money from your parents? Do you feel worthy to receive something you may feel you did not directly earn? Does their money come to you at a steep price or with strings attached?

Examine your relationship to money and inheritance even further. Are you saving an inheritance for your children? Do you save your money for your children to ease their financial path, or do you live in the moment and enjoy spending it on yourself without guilt? Do you continue to focus on amassing greater monetary wealth, even though you already have enough for your retirement and your children's financial needs?

Getting your will in order will help you to determine what you want to do with your money. You are responsible for yourself and then your loved ones. When you go on an airplane, the flight attendants instruct you to put the oxygen mask on yourself first and then on your children. If you do not provide for yourself, you have less to provide for your children. If you withhold fulfillment from yourself, then your children inherit money associated with your sense of self-denial.

Sometimes people feel resistant about receiving a monetary inheritance from their parents. They may feel the money is tainted with bitterness and resentment. Frequently, family members fight over their inheritance, reopening old wounds or creating new ones. At times, forgiveness and healing accompany an inheritance. Then there are times when there is no financial inheritance because there was never any money to save in the first place.

• • •

How has your inheritance affected your life?

I was born in the United States during the second half of the Twentieth Century, a time and place of prosperity and opportunity. It was an era of technological innovation, modern convenience and freedom of expression. I am so grateful for this aspect of my inheritance, because I know that my life was much easier than it would have been otherwise.

I was born a male, which came with its own set of inherited beliefs. I inherited the belief that being the sole provider for my family demonstrated my masculinity. I inherited the belief that I had to be tough and fight for what I want because that is what men do, that showing my feelings was a sign of weakness.

I was born into a Jewish family. I learned that people hated Jews and, in many cases, wanted to kill them just because they were Jews. I was born into this tribe that has been on the run for 5,000 years. I learned that, as a Jew, I was one step away from persecution at all times. Even if I changed my name, they could still find me. And if they did, they could take everything away from me. They could take all of my material wealth, like they did to my ancestors.

Pretty heavy stuff to pass on to your son!

I inherited the beliefs of someone born in the Depression Era to an immigrant family. I inherited the belief that life is full of struggle, even though the Depression was in the past and I was a full-fledged U.S. citizen.

Even though I learned that, as a Jew, I could not have security, I did learn that I could have money. Having money was as close as I could get to security. "Be a doctor or a lawyer —you'll make good money," I was told. Everything I was taught in school or saw on TV supported the same message. "You gotta have money. It's the golden rule: If you have the gold, you make the rule."

With the inherited belief that the man is the provider for the family, I was emotionally challenged when my dad experienced a period of unemployment during the recession of

1973. I witnessed his suffering and sense of emasculation. Feeling my father's pain and suffering around money left a deep impression. I took on my father's pain and suffering as my own—as an inheritance of the moment.

At age sixteen, I took matters into my own hands. I got a job at a local supermarket as a stock boy. I felt that I needed to contribute money to offset whatever financial burden I was placing on the family. On one hand, unloading the trucks and stocking the shelves with Spam were two of the last things on Earth I wanted to do. On the other hand, I was grateful for the opportunity to earn a portion of my keep.

Eventually I got laid off because I was the most recent hire in the union shop. I got a chance to feel firsthand disappointment and a sense of failure surrounding money. That experience increased my resolve to break through this inheritance concerning money being the source of my self-esteem and masculinity.

Beyond inherited beliefs, did you ever inherit any money from your ancestors?

When my grandfather died, he left me an inheritance of $4,000, earmarked for my education. By the time I entered college, my inheritance had grown to $10,000. I decided that if I invested the original $4,000 dollars in the stock market, I could fast track my dream of making big money.

I lost it all!

My grandfather's wish came true. It *did* go towards my education. I learned about the relationship of risk and reward. I applied myself with greater dedication to my education and to my profession as a result of that experience. I also learned that, because I did not earn it directly, I had less respect for that money. I had the inherited belief that I had to achieve financial success for myself, not have it handed to me.

When my Dad passed away, he left me nothing through his last will and testament. He did leave me a video recorded one month before his passing. He told our family on that video how important it is to love life passionately and to love each other. He also stressed the importance of family in one's life. There was standing room only at his funeral—almost a thousand people were there to pay their respects. People whose lives my father touched in one way or another through his love of life and his love of others. That is my inheritance. Thank you, Dad. I love you, too.

So it sounds like the most valuable thing you inherited is love. It seems as though love really is the true treasure. Imagine what the world would be if everyone placed the highest value on love. It is really amazing to know that through my free will I can choose what inherited beliefs I want to adopt. So much of the world has adopted the belief that war is an inherent state of the human condition. Through my free will, I can reject this belief and choose to pass on to my children that love and compassion can resolve conflict.

How has your inheritance shaped your life?

What aspects of your inheritance do you treasure?

What aspects of your inheritance burden you?

Are you willing to receive your divine inheritance of prosperity, miracles and boundless joy…

…right now?

Ownership

Through ownership, you choose the

self-identity that unlocks your inner wealth.

Ownership

New Year's Day. It was a fine day, this new day of a new year, to get in the hot tub. The visionary and the achiever soaked to the bones and were awestruck by what a powerfully unpredictable year it had been. New Year's Day has traditionally been a day of 'the will' in the making of resolutions and wish lists for the year to come. It is also a day of inheritance—a product of all previous years. The visionary saw beyond his inheritance as he proclaimed that this was the year of owning his dreams.

What do you really own?

You seem to own things...things you want.

A car.

A house.

A mutual fund.

Some things you dream of owning.

A new car.

A bigger house.

A soaring mutual fund.

In actuality, you don't own material things.

You are merely renting them.

Everything in the material world is temporal and can disappear in an instant.

Every thing...including your body.

In time everything turns to dust...

While you are the temporary custodian of your material possessions, you are responsible for them. Whether you are driving a car you own, rent or borrow, you are responsible for driving it safely. And yet, even though you are responsible for driving your car safely, you have no control over the ultimate disposition of that car. The car might be stolen or totaled in a split second. This is beyond your control.

So much is beyond your control. Your spouse, children and employees are beyond your control. You cannot control what they think or do, no matter how much you may want to. The most you can hope to do is to inspire and influence them.

SO MUCH IS BEYOND YOUR CONTROL. WHAT YOU CAN CONTROL ARE YOUR ACTIONS AND REACTIONS.

What can you control? What can you own?

You can control and own your actions and reactions to the world around you.

What determines your actions and reactions?

Your self-identity. This is the lens through which you view life. The color and clarity of the lens are based on inherited beliefs and feelings. You have a full spectrum of possibilities for how you perceive yourself—ranging from self-love to self-hate. You alone are responsible for choosing the self-identity that best fits the realization of your dreams. If your self-identity is one of a starving artist, this may derail your dreams of becoming a rich and successful one.

You own your self-identity. In fact, you create it.

In this moment, go back to your will. What do you want to experience in your life right now? What do you want to create for your future?

You have a vast inheritance of images and concepts from which to shape or completely recreate your self-identity. You may be in the habit of identifying with images and concepts that other people have projected onto you. You may have taken ownership of thoughts and beliefs that are imposed on you or need not be yours.

YOU ALONE ARE RESPONSIBLE FOR CHOOSING THE SELF-IDENTITY THAT BEST FITS THE REALIZATION OF YOUR DREAMS.

Who do you want to be? A person someone else wants you to be? A person you think you should be based on an old set of beliefs? Or a person true to their own nature?

Own your *true* self-identity. Claim from your divine inheritance what you need to actualize your dreams. Seize the ideals and virtues that are aligned to the highest vision of who you are!

Inside, there is no limit to what you can own. Yet you may own things that restrict you—such as certain attitudes about love, intimacy, money and power. Reassess these beliefs to determine whether or not they support your will. They may be merely old ideas inherited from others, in which case, you may wish to trade them in for ones that are more liberating, ones that sustain you in living the life you want to live.

So you are saying that no one is stuck with the life they have, and that we can trade in old ideas about ourselves for new ones like trading in a used car. How is this possible for someone who may have a lifetime of low self-esteem?

The lifetime of low self-esteem exists entirely in the past. To be in the present and release this deeply ingrained self-image that does not support you, you may need to forgive yourself and others right now for all the moments of pain and suffering you have ever created or experienced. Despite all the emotional hardship of the past, you have somehow survived to get to this moment. You can claim a new and healthier self-identity right now with a keen sense of appreciation: because you know one less desirable alternative all too well.

Return to your will. Do you want to continue on a path of low self-esteem, or do you want to trade it all in right now for a self-identity that offers greater inner peace and self-worth? It may seem like a big leap to go from one existence to another in an instant. You can self-manage the pace of your transition into a new self-identity. Your will is free.

At times, you may feel unworthy to achieve what you really want. The voice of your *inner self-critic* may tell you that you are not good enough, not smart enough or not lovable enough. These thoughts are a product of other people's projections and judgments that you have internalized. They are the product of inheritance. Nothing more, nothing less.

The inner self-critic feels like part of the self-identity. People can actually believe that this is who they are. Someone who was told at an impressionable age that they were stupid and would never amount to anything, could believe that good grades and a lucrative career are beyond their grasp. In assuming this limiting self-image, their dreams become impossible to fulfill.

When you own the qualities of life that support your dreams, you close the gap that separates you from what you really want.

When you embody higher values such as love, honor and compassion, you can access the creative energy latent inside you. These virtues are your own and cannot be taken from you.

To embody higher values, you may need to let go of certain habits and patterns of behavior. If you wish to own the quality of compassion for others, you first need to have compassion for yourself. This requires replacing self-judgment with forgiveness and self-appreciation, so that you are able to nurture yourself in times of despair. Once you can be more compassionate for yourself, you can then feel this emotion for others.

It seems to me that most people are attached to their self-identity. They have projected a certain persona, and seem bound to appear as others expect them to be. How does a person with a reputation as a pessimist, for example, all of a sudden appear as an optimist without everyone doubting their sincerity?

You are under no obligation to be someone you are not, even if that means disappointing or confusing people. Our inheritance is laden with beliefs and actions designed to meet other people's expectations. Just because someone expects you to be a pessimist doesn't mean that you need to meet his or her expectations. Even though you may have created certain expectations through past beliefs and actions, you have free will to modify or radically alter your self-identity at any time. Your historical pessimism may simply be an inherited attitude about life —an attitude that, in your heart, you want to change.

Realistically, it may take some period of time for people to accept "the new you." The key is to continue to be true to yourself and sustain your new self-identity. This may require self-love and sensitivity to the people who are used to viewing you a certain way. As you do so, your relationships will change to reflect who you have become.

YOU ARE UNDER NO OBLIGATION TO BE SOMEONE YOU ARE NOT, EVEN IF THAT MEANS DISAPPOINTING OR CONFUSING PEOPLE.

You can become attached to your self-identity, even if it no longer serves you. You may feel grief with your transformation. For instance, when you let go of the self-critic, you may feel loss or emptiness. It may feel strange, even foreign, not to hear that voice that tells you, "You are not good enough, you are not lovable enough, you are not worthy of contentment." By letting go of who you think you are—especially aspects of your inheritance that inhibit you—you are free to recreate yourself into who you want to be.

This sounds like a corporate re-branding. Do I actually walk around with a t-shirt stating "New and Improved?"

The image that you convey to the world is created from the inside out through your own self-identity. This does apply to corporations as well. Corporations take ownership of their self-identity, shaping it to achieve their mission. Adopting the belief that its greatest assets are its reputation and employees, a corporation disowns the belief that it is a purely legal and inanimate entity. Instead, its self-image encompasses many human hearts and minds dedicated to a common goal. After all, even corporate makeovers are part of our inheritance.

EVERYTHING IN THE OUTER WORLD IS PERPETUALLY SHIFTING, TRANSFORMING AND SUBJECT TO CHANGE AT ANY MOMENT!

Change is inevitable, anyway. Everything in the outer world is perpetually shifting, transforming and changing shape. Even your wealth is constantly fluctuating. Stock worth thousands today could be worth hundreds tomorrow.

Everything you own in the outer world is subject to change at any moment!

And, yet, this moment has never existed before!

In this moment, pick and choose from the totality of your inheritance the beliefs that support your dreams. Claim ownership of who you really want to be. It is time to own the virtues that will stimulate greater joy, flow and prosperity in your life. It is time to breathe these virtues into your deepest self.

Embody them!

Own them!

Go back to your will!

When your will is in order, then you can clearly identify what you need to own to support you. For example, if your will is to become financially successful, you need to own a set of beliefs that serve you in this quest. This may also call for releasing beliefs that have inhibited you from achieving financial wealth today, such as the belief that money and power are addictive.

Claim the principles of money that support its attraction to you. Possess a complete set of ideals that are consistent with creating the wealth you want. Own the belief that you are worthy of material wealth. In order to achieve financial security, you do need to believe you are worthy. It is necessary to feel that you have value, and that you offer value in return for money.

Can you give me an example?

Even if you are a starving artist, you can become a millionaire. Others have. Their success is part of your inheritance. Every rags-to-riches story is your inheritance. Claim *their* success as *your* potential destiny. Disown the idea that it takes money to make money. Uphold the notion that your art is an expression of love—as is money. The concept that money can be an expression of love is also part of your inheritance. There need not be a separation between the two. Own the belief that your art is an expression of your love—your very being. That is worth its weight in gold.

If I am a starving artist, what virtues do I need to own to fulfill my destiny as a wealthy artist?

Patience, dedication and courage are three qualities that may enable you to reach your goal. You may need to feel that you do have the talent to break through the barrier of rejection and rise to the top. You may need to feel how sick and tired you are of waiting for your success. You may have to let go of your attachment to the pot of gold at the end of the rainbow, and begin to enjoy each color and shade along the way. By enjoying the journey without attachment, you may find your way to your goal a lot easier. Your pot of gold may appear in an unexpected way.

How do you gain ownership of virtuous qualities such as patience, dedication and courage?

The first step to owning virtue is to return to your will. If your dream is to make money through your passion as an artist, feel the purity and strength of this desire. Sift through your vast inheritance to identify the thoughts, beliefs and virtues that support you in the achievement of this goal. In this case, to own patience, a virtuous quality that you believe enhances your success, become aware of when it is absent.

To be more patient, you will need to practice patience as a skill. Notice when you are impatient. Become aware of your breath. Shift your breath into a deep, relaxed rhythm. Using an affirmation such as "I now let go of time, I will get there when I get there," may help you to feel a deeper sense of patience.

Once you are feeling patient, you begin to let go of a need to control time. In that state of detachment from instant gratification, you are free to be in the timelessness of your passion for artistic expression. Dedication naturally flows from your passion. Through your dedication, your artistry has the time and space to evolve into its greatest forms of manifestation.

You may feel fear from time to time. It is only natural. Fear may even be your ally alerting you to potential danger. And, at times, it may be an old inherited response that prevents you from living your dreams. So, as you have free will, you are free to invite in your love of life in its entirety as well.

Courage is feeling your fears and rising above them to take right action. Your passion and love for what you hold most sacred, such as living the life of your dreams, override your fear of loss or failure. You can summon courage into your body when you arise, when you are in the shower, when you are stuck in traffic. When you go to sleep at night, you can embody or begin to embody these virtues. In time, courage becomes embodied within you, not an attribute separate from you.

Start right now.

Fan the flames of your burning desires.

Feel yourself breathing passion throughout your body.

Feel courage flowing through your veins, inspiring you to pierce the veil of limiting, fear-based beliefs you may have inherited from your parents, teachers and society.

As an artist, live a life of richness and passion. What you feel on the inside projects to the outside. Feel your wealth inside and it will show up in your outer life. You can bet your inheritance on it!

INSIDE, THERE IS NO LIMIT TO WHAT YOU CAN OWN.

It just may not show up the way you think. You may end up finding your abstract designs on sheets and pillowcases instead of canvas.

Anything is possible!

Be open!

Place no limits on what you own!

Tell me about how you have owned virtues and how they directly related to your monetary success?

I was a stockbroker who was committed to accumulating financial wealth. My compensation was commission-based, which means I was paid to produce transactions. The more trades I generated, the more money I made—irrespective of whether the client made money or not. Sometimes the best investment strategy in the stock market was inaction. In other words, sometimes no transaction was the best transaction for the client—even though for me this meant I would not get paid.

After a couple of years, my discomfort rose to intolerable levels. I needed to restructure my business in accordance with my desire to be in alignment with my clients' financial objectives. I adopted a structure in which I was paid a percentage of my investor's profits. This way I only made money if they did. If they lost money, I would not get paid again until their loss was fully recouped.

I had to quit being a stockbroker to go off commission-based compensation. I needed to claim ownership of virtues that would support my success. I claimed ownership of courage, faith, honesty and integrity as the cornerstones of my new endeavor. I raised money from my brokerage clients to start the new venture.

With this new compensation structure in place, they were no longer my clients — they were my partners. They owned a stake in my success. By being paid a percentage of the profits they made — I owned a stake in their success. Although I no longer own this business, I continue to own courage, faith, honesty and integrity as essential attributes of my self-identity.

Even though money can buy you practically anything in the material world, no matter how much money you have, you can't buy virtues. Your virtue can only be owned from the inside out.

Do you own your actions
and reactions....

And take responsibility for
what you create in the world?

Can you take responsibility for creating your own self-identity?

Who do you want to be…
right now?

Value

Measure your self-worth by

the weight of your values.

Value

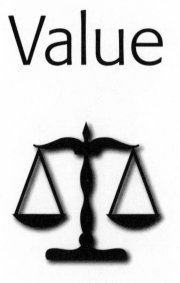

The rain was unrelenting, like their spirits. The visionary and achiever were off on their weekly walk through the redwood trees; the sodden canopy of lush green became the ideal setting to discuss the birth of their book. Everything felt alive; ferns thriving in moisture reflected minds fertile with creativity.

The visionary and achiever were at a turning point, the point in which they were claiming authorship of their ideas as well as ownership of their destiny. As they walked further into the forest their discussion deepened into the value of writing a book about inner security in insecure times.

What is value?

Value is how you measure what you own.

You value your material possessions.

Your car.

>Your house.

>>Your stock portfolio.

You value the virtues that you own.

Your inner strength.

>Your passion for life.

>>Your creative power.

You value other people for their contribution to your life.

Your family.

>Your friends.

>>Your community.

What role does value play in the world of finance?

In the stock market, when you buy a stock—you own shares in a company. The value of the enterprise fluctuates through its stock price. One goal of corporate management is to maximize the shareholder's value. The goal of the investor is to own stocks that will increase in value. When a company takes strategic action steps to raise its stock price to more accurately reflect the underlying worth of its enterprise, it is referred to in the financial world as "unlocking the value."

How can I unlock my value?

You can unlock the value and meaning of your life through discovering your deepest desires and by owning the qualities that support their realization. Take stock in your true self-identity and discover the life path with most value to you. Value is in the eye of the beholder. Now is the time to clarify the values that give your life its highest purpose and reveal the richness of your own inner treasure.

When you identify and live your life purpose—the highest purpose for your presence on Earth—you unlock infinite value in your life. You unleash a positive energy with which you magnetize the achievement of your goals. You can actualize your dreams, and more, simply because your intent, desire and will are all aligned to fulfill your reasons for being in this lifetime. Imagine that you have a clearly defined standard by which you can measure all your actions and reactions qualitatively. You can ask yourself every day, "Is this action consistent with my life purpose?" Achievement occurs through flow and inspiration with a sense of self-satisfaction and gratitude.

Contrast this process of achievement with another prevailing perspective on success, especially financial success. Many people have accumulated money through insecurity, not inner security. Motivation can arise from a fear of failure, a fear of insufficiency or a perceived need to prove worthiness. Achievement in these cases is experienced as a struggle, met with inner and outer resistance. This path to "success" is limited to the outer world and, therefore, feels unfulfilling and incomplete.

Value is a screening process to assess your alignment with your will. Through ownership, you get to choose your self-identity.

Through value, you are able to realize how precious your life truly is. Value is what you do with what you own.

SELF-WORTH IS THE SUM OF THE QUALITIES YOU OWN. NET WORTH IS THE SUM OF THE QUANTITIES.

Does what you own have meaning to you, and is it congruent with your heart's desires? In answering these questions you are measuring your self-worth. Self-worth is the sum of the qualities you own. net worth is the sum of the quantities. When you own virtues and ideals, the attributes and principles of the highest quality, you increase your sense of self-worth.

Think about how significant your life is. Consider how much you impact others through your actions and your very being. Your will, your inheritance, what you own and the value of your life are all immense—beyond measure.

Yet, in our society, it is through money that we frequently measure value.

How do you explain why athletes and entertainers get paid so much? Do they really offer us that much value?

We pay athletes a fortune because they offer us tremendous value. They offer us the thrill of possibility in the moment. Anything is possible in sports. The underdog can beat the favorite. Individual human achievement in any given moment can amaze us. Athletes make us feel more alive by engaging us in present time.

Entertainers make us laugh, make us cry and invite us to experience the whole spectrum of emotions. All of our senses are stimulated through their passionate self-expression.

Ultimately, these people get paid so much money because they do make us feel more alive. That has extreme value. By no means is this a justification for the disparity of income that exists today.

After all, money does not always accurately reflect value.

You can say that again! How about a childcare worker and the value they offer society? You know how much your children mean to you! A childcare worker can get paid less than a parking lot attendant, yet you trust them with the well being of your child. As a society, do we value our children less than our cars?

Clearly, money is not always an accurate measurement of value. If an imbalance persists for an extended period of time, you can experience a real loss. Creating and maintaining a balanced relationship between money and value begins with each one of us. It starts by going within.

THE OUTER REFLECTS THE INNER: THE GREATER YOUR SELF-WORTH, THE MORE HIGHLY OTHERS WILL VALUE YOU.

As the outer reflects the inner, the greater certainty you have as to your own self-worth, the more highly others will value you. This dictates that you claim your value as well as your values. If you do not value yourself, others do not value you either. There is a collective inherited belief that "you get what you pay for." The less you value what you offer, the less other people receive from you.

For example, you are a consultant with twenty years experience behind you. You are paid by the hour for your services. Your time is measured with money. You have achieved competence in your field. Notwithstanding your accomplishments, your self-esteem is low and you have persistent financial issues. You have conflicts surrounding prosperity.

Because you have a low self-image, you find it difficult to set your hourly rate consistent with your level of competence. You may be offering your services below their true value. On one hand, you are offering your prospective clients a substantial bargain. On the other hand, they may perceive you as incompetent because you are projecting a devalued self-worth.

How do you break a pattern that no longer serves you?

Go back to your will. Feel deeply what it is that you want and love. If you want and love a greater sense of financial stability and professional advancement, then feel the intensity of that desire. Sift through your inheritance to discover the beliefs, virtues and steps of action you need to realize your will. Claim and breathe life into your new self. Reassess your value in this moment. Feel the power of your will as you realize the value of what you offer. With your renewed sense of self, you have the power to re-establish your value and raise your rates accordingly. Through your expansion of self-worth you are increasing your net-worth.

Your time and energy are your most valuable resources. Because time is so precious, what you do with your time is one of the most important issues you face.

You cannot own time.

You can create time.

THROUGH VALUE, YOU ARE ABLE TO REALIZE HOW PRECIOUS YOUR LIFE TRULY IS. VALUE IS WHAT YOU DO WITH EACH MOMENT.

The same is true of money. You don't really own it; you create it with decisions and actions. Money and time are partners.

How is that so?

Investment theory explains how to adequately value a company and, therefore, how to measure its worth via its stock price. The financial principle is called "the time value of money." The premise is that the value of an enterprise today is determined by the cash flows it generates now and in the future that are available to its owners, the stockholders.

Financial theory also holds that there is infinite money. Theoretically, there is no limit to our financial wealth. Either individually or collectively, there are no limits to how much money you can have. Theoretically, that is.

You are on the Earth in your body for a finite time. Your time and energy are your most precious resources because they are limited in supply and they are in demand.

What is the value of your life? What is the monetary value of your time? What is the monetary value of looking into your beloved's eyes with love and devotion? What is the monetary value of look-ing into your children's eyes, knowing love, seeing love, feeling love that is beyond speech? What is the monetary value of look-ing into the mirror and loving who and what you see?

These moments are priceless. All moments can be priceless, as rich as we can possibly perceive.

It is time...to value this moment, to honor this moment. It is time to make time for the activities that reward you the most—the activities that enrich your life...art, music, sports, eating, travel, connecting.

It is time to maximize the return on all your investments—especially to maximize the return on your most dear asset: your time. Time with your self, with the people you love, time to make this world a more abundant experience for all. Time to maximize the value of your life.

•　•　•

So what I am beginning to see is that when you know what you want, clear the barriers of inherit-ed beliefs, begin to own your value and value what you own, your self-worth increases. What role did self-worth play in your professional life and in determining your net-worth?

Early in my career as a stockbroker, I struggled because I had no sales experience and no client base. I was develop-ing my client base through cold calling—an experience largely fraught with rejection. I had to pick up the phone thirty to forty times a day and advise strangers what to do with their hard-earned capital. At least seven out of ten calls ended with a request that I not call back. Dismissal often took the form of an abrupt dial tone or, in some cases, rude, unprovoked personal attacks.

I had to own the virtues of self-love, perseverance and diligence to survive in this business. Without my sense of self-worth, I would have changed careers in a heartbeat.

One day I cold-called an elderly gentleman. He said he had just invested $100,000 in a tax-free bond and was not going to transact that day. I asked him how often he made such investments, and he told me he did so about once a month. At that point, I became dedicated to calling him every few weeks for the rest of my career, with the intent of securing him as my client.

After several months of conversation without transaction, he confided in me that he had sold his family business to a large consumer products company. As luck or fate had it, several months later that company became the subject of takeover rumors. I called security analysts, money managers and scoured the financial publications for as much information as I could find about the company and its potential value to a suitor. I communicated to this gentleman anything I saw, heard or knew on a timely basis. He rewarded my diligence by selling $5,000,000 worth of stock through me.

Through this multi-million dollar transaction, I had broken the ice into the world of high finance. I owned my competency in our relationship. I revalued myself to a higher standard accordingly. With this new attitude of increased self-confidence, I attracted more high net worth clients. I was in complete alignment with my deepest heartfelt desires to be financially successful. The virtues I owned had value. I had both increased self-worth and net worth as a result.

•   •   •

My Values

I value who I am and what I stand for.

I value my family, friends and community.

I value love and my ability to feel and express it.

I value nature, in all of its splendor and beauty.

I value the physical health and senses that allow me to experience the richness of this lifetime.

I value my life.

I am very inspired to imagine what the world could become if people clarified their values. If they were able to take inventory of what they value most, they would most likely discover that love is the highest standard, and a life of love is what we value most.

What do you value most
in your life?

How is your self-worth related to your net-worth?

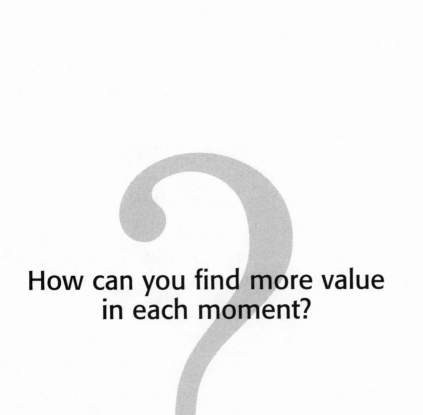

How can you find more value in each moment?

What is your self…worth?

Trust

Trust is the foundation of

your infinite wealth.

Trust

The winter rains yielded fields of wild lupines. The visionary and achiever drove up the road to view a ranch the achiever was in contract to buy. They got out of the truck and began to walk the soggy land.

The achiever talked about how his external life was rapidly taking on new shape. He trusted that everything was perfect. The visionary reflected about his experience co-authoring a book with his buddy. He spoke of how the blending of their two voices into one harmonious voice drew them into deeper levels of trust within themselves and each other.

What do you trust?

Trust is where you store your value.

A trust account is a place for safekeeping. We each have a personal trust in which we place our values.

The greater you value what you own, the greater you can trust in it.

If integrity has great value to you...

> you can trust in the integrity you own.

If dedication has great value to you...

> you can trust in the dedication you own.

If love has great value to you...

> you can trust in your love.

Trust begins with trusting in your self.

You already have established a trust in yourself with every breath that you take. You do not need to think or concern yourself about breathing. You just breathe. Your body has its own innate intelligence. This is a form of trust, a form of inner security.

Consider how you are developing your sense of inner security.

You are establishing your will. Your will is enormous!

You are claiming your inheritance. Your inheritance is vast!

You are declaring ownership of your self-identity.

You are discovering your greater value.

All of this adds up to substantial personal power. Can you trust yourself with this power?

Your inherited beliefs may associate power with corruption. You may associate power with abuse. You may associate power with violence. Even altruistic use of power may have had unintended consequences. In many cases, the abuse of power is associated with money.

Can you trust that money and power will not corrupt you, or abuse you, or that you will not be abused by it? Can you trust that the desire to make money will not override your basic values and virtues? After all, think of what people have done in the name of money.

Lied?

Cheated?

Murdered?

TRUST IS WHERE YOU STORE YOUR VALUE AND VALUES. THE GREATER YOUR SELF-WORTH, THE MORE YOU CAN TRUST IN YOURSELF.

When people are corrupted by their hunger for money, they violate trust in the virtues of compassion, integrity and honesty. As a result, they mistrust each other and create a tainted impression of money. They contaminate the essence of money, leaving many to rationalize that money is the root of all evil. No wonder so many lives are burdened with money worries and trust issues!

Trust, therefore, is the cornerstone of finance.

Trust must be essential to our financial system. After all, the motto "In God We Trust" is imprinted on every dollar bill. Have you ever considered the meaning of "In God We Trust" on our money? What significance, if any, does it have for you?

As a money manager, I participated regularly in multi-million dollar stock transactions without considering this motto. It doesn't take a student of money flows to observe that the awareness of "In God We Trust" seems to be absent from most financial exchanges.

If you think about it, it is logical that the inscription "In God We Trust" does appear on every U.S. coin and paper currency by design. By invoking the name of God on our currency, perhaps our forefathers were trying to inspire us to raise our consciousness in all financial transactions—so that money is used for its highest possible purpose for the sake of our country, as well as for personal benefit. If the word and concept of "God" does not work for any of us, we can insert an "o" into the phrase, revising it to "In Good We Trust."

The "We" of this inspiration refers to the person with the money and the person who offers the product or service in exchange. This is important because it does take at least two people to agree that money has value. If you were lost alone in the woods with a one thousand dollar bill, its value would be reduced to personal warmth or hygiene.

The "Trust" is essential because without trust, no one would accept paper money in exchange for goods and services. Without trust, there is no credit extended or loans offered. Without trust, no one invests in the stock market.

Clearly, trust has been violated in the stock market through the experience of failed corporate giants, dishonorable business practices and even questionable government leadership.

How do we repair trust? Will stiffer jail sentences for corporate executives suffice, or do we need a higher standard upon which to rebuild trust?

Punishment usually does not rebuild trust. It must start within each individual...starting with you. It is vital to remember that trust lives within the core of your being.

By being on the path of inner security, the rebuilding of trust has already begun. It starts with your will and the desire to live the life that you want and love. It continues by scanning your inheritance and becoming aware of the assets and liabilities you have inherited. You then are able to choose your self-identity and the virtues you want to own—to experience and embody. You have a renewed sense of self-worth based on the values you cherish. You can trust that they do have infinite value.

You are establishing your personal trust account in which you store your value. Just like your will—this is yours and yours alone. No one can take it away; there are no limits.

Trust may be the biggest issue facing people today because no one knows what the future will bring.

Trust exists only in the moment.

Trust and uncertainty are directly related.

Many times you are in the position of making choices with no certainty as to the outcome. This is why it is important to go into your heart and gut to trust in your self. This may be challenging if you have strong memories of trust being violated. Each of us has experienced varying degrees of broken trust—either emotionally, mentally, physically or spiritually. Distrust is projected onto money as a consequence.

TRUST EXISTS ONLY IN THE MOMENT.

Anyone who has filed for personal bankruptcy most likely has faced trust issues associated with money. Each one of us has a unique relationship to trust and money.

For example, the consultant who is upwardly revising her hourly rate may have a trust issue. She may feel that her value will not be acceptable to her current and prospective clients. In going through her will, inheritance and issues of ownership, she has established a greater sense of value for the services she offers. She can trust that her competency warrants the rate increase.

The consultant may encounter resistance to her rate increase, which could result in some client attrition. She then may need to go back to her will to realize how much she wants to be valued appropriately for her services. The loss of a few clients may actually be consistent with her desired results. Her ownership of greater self-worth is the basis for her unwavering trust—in herself.

Do you know what it feels like to trust yourself?

There is a sense of comfort, peace and contentment.

Trust in self is a cornerstone of inner security.

What is the difference between faith and trust?

Faith is the deepest form of trust. Faith goes beyond hope. You may hope that you will succeed in a new endeavor, yet you may have some doubts based on either past evidence of failure or merely a lack of experience. Faith goes beyond doubt. Your faith can be tested, questioned and shaken to its core through events that are beyond your control—no matter what personal tragedies you may experience.

TRUST IN SELF IS A CORNERSTONE OF INNER SECURITY. FAITH IS THE DEEPEST FORM OF TRUST.

Your faith is a portal to your highest self-realization. Faith is the certainty that lies within you amidst life's uncertain circumstances. With faith, the concept of "anything is possible" opens up a field of infinite possibilities that exceeds our rational expectations. Without trust, we dare not venture beyond what we can predict or control, thereby limiting our possible range of outcomes accordingly.

It is through trust and faith that we take our inner security out into the world. With a developed sense of inner security, trust and faith enable our limitless assets such as will and inheritance to project into our environment—to create infinite wealth.

When you have faith, you are fully aware that whatever you are experiencing in the moment is perfect for your personal transformation. In this way, you have the freedom to transcend life circumstances and not limit your self-identity to them. With faith, you are actually letting go into the mystery of life.

Faith and trust go beyond your mind and emotions. Just think and feel how much you trust your body's own innate intelligence. When you go to sleep at night, you trust that you will wake up in the morning regenerated. Your body's innate intelligence even knows how to keep you safe. It knows how to secrete the proper hormones in an instant to keep you out of harm's way. Already, so many of your unconscious and intentional experiences throughout the day are infused with trust - expand your trust with even a greater awareness that you can deepen your sense of inner security even further.

• • •

You have spent your adult life seeking security through money. How could you trust that walking away from your livelihood was the right thing to do?

Leaving my investment firm and releasing a dream I had for so long was one of the hardest decisions of my life—until it became one of the easiest decisions of my life. The prospect of liquidating my business conjured up feelings of failure and fear of judgment. It raised one of the deepest issues of my life—how am I going to provide for my family financially?

I knew I no longer had the same self-identity I had when I started the company five years prior. I was a money manager in the stock market. It was more than what I did; it was who I was.

As I looked deeper into my life, I discovered I had desires for my life both professionally and personally that superseded the dream of running the firm I had founded. My deepest wish was to experience a sense of security independent from net worth, especially in the moments when I was losing money. I also wanted to explore how to provide for my family while expressing what was truly in my heart.

I had no idea what form this new career path would take. Even with the knowledge and desire to step into a new life, the uncertainty as to what this would look like drew me into bouts of self-doubt. Additionally, I was unclear as to what skills I had other than managing money. I had to let go of my mind and the doubts that occupied it. I needed to go into my heart. I had to let go and trust the uncertainty.

I was in the void!

What comfort I did have was that I knew I was being true to myself. I was trusting in the value of that. I was trusting in the value of my courage, of my self-love and of the purity of my heart. Through this trust I was able to take the action step of letting go of my business—and I knew there were no money back guarantees.

• • •

My trust

I trust in God.

I trust that there are no limits to how deeply I can feel love.

I trust that there are no limits to how deeply you can feel love.

I trust in my value and values.

I trust in the virtues of self-love, compassion, courage, integrity, perseverance and humility, and in my dedication to embody them.

I trust in my body wisdom: in my instincts, in my intuition, in my heart.

I trust that my needs will always be met somehow.

I trust that I will always be the best father and husband that I possibly can.

I trust my dedication to being true to myself.

I trust that I can accept the personal power of being who I am without abusing it or being corrupted by it.

I trust that writing this book brings me closer to realizing my deepest heart's desires.

I trust that anything is possible, including living my dreams.

With my will in order, my divine inheritance in hand, my ownership of inner wealth and enhanced self-worth, I have one huge personal trust account to take out into the world!

What do you trust?

What do you mistrust?

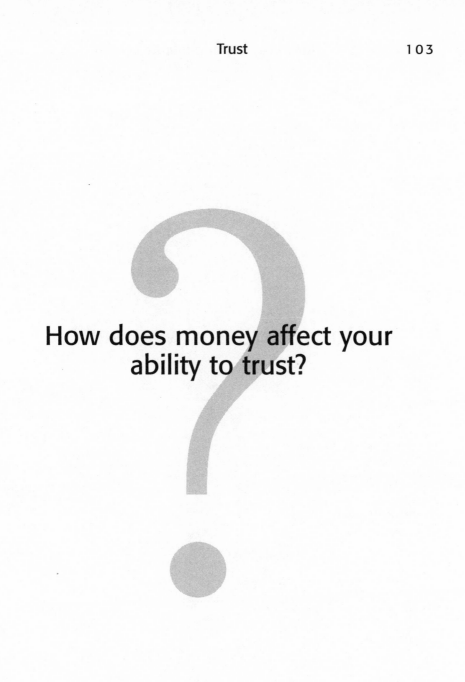

How does money affect your ability to trust?

Do you trust in yourself?

Allowance

Give yourself an allowance to

actualize your dreams.

Allowance

What is so wonderful about spring is that everyone seems to come out of hibernation. The air was fragrant as the two authors took their children to the neighborhood park. As the children ran, climbed and rejoiced in the splendor of the moment, the visionary and achiever allowed themselves to view their lives through the eyes of a child.

As they talked, they discovered that their act of writing the book was a form of play as well. Play with words, play with ideas and play in the field of infinite possibilities. This was an opportunity for both men to trust and allow the book to be a product of play.

What is your allowance?

Did you receive an allowance as a child?

If you did, how did it feel to receive it?

Were you excited?

Did you save it in a piggy bank?

Did you spend it on gum?

Did it feel like it was enough?

Do you feel you deserve one now?

Can you give yourself an allowance to live your dreams?

Your allowance to live your dreams is built on trust in yourself. Through allowance, you begin to take action steps to manifest your heart's desires into your everyday life. The greater you trust in your value, the bigger your *inner-trust account*. The bigger your *inner-trust account*, the more of an allowance you have to give yourself.

Allowance is a short-term expression of trust.

You do not allow what you do not trust.

If you do not trust your romantic partner, you do not allow for greater intimacy in the relationship. You do not allow yourself to be vulnerable, to hurt. If greater trust is built over time with your partner, you allow for greater depth and closeness between you.

It is time to give yourself an allowance based on the trust that you have established in your self. Your trust is comprised of the values and virtues you choose to own and embody. You have carefully screened and selected these ideals from the entirety of your rich inheritance. Your will is strong and coherent. You have claimed ownership of who you want to be, and it is time to take action.

Your allowance can be your first step, and it can be a baby step.

ALLOWANCE IS AN ACTION STEP IN THE DIRECTION OF YOUR DREAMS. EACH STEP IS BASED ON TRUST IN YOURSELF.

If you want to re-establish a healthy relationship to your physical body, your allowance may be as simple as a new workout routine. If you want to reduce the stress of being in front of your computer for eight straight hours, give yourself an allowance to eat your lunch away from your desk. If you want to express the feelings that are deep in your heart to someone you love, give yourself an allowance to write them a love letter. If you want to discover your deeper spiritual nature, you can give yourself an allowance to sit in silence.

Through allowance, you expand your life into new horizons, you begin to have a new set of actions in your life. You can own these actions and value them more highly than previous ones. As you find more value in your actions you increase your self-worth. As you increase your self-worth through these new experiences, you have even more trust from which to source more allowances. In making time to read this book—you are giving yourself an allowance to go even deeper into your self-awareness.

How can you utilize the process of allowance beyond the day to day? How about giving yourself an allowance once a month to go a little further outside the parameters of your daily life? Try engaging in one activity a month completely new to you. This activity or experience can be in alignment with your values and beyond the boundaries of your routine.

Once you become comfortable with the daily and monthly allowance you give yourself, you develop even greater trust in this process. Give yourself permission to push the envelope of personal experience even further. How about doing something once a year that is life altering? Give yourself an experience that is truly unforgettable. If you want to go beyond your wildest dreams, start with your wild and wilder dreams. The possibilities are endless!

GIVE YOURSELF PERMISSION TO PUSH THE ENVELOPE OF PERSONAL EXPERIENCE EVEN FURTHER.

You talk about giving yourself an allowance. How about receiving an allowance?

In the outer world, an allowance can imply that there is a form of hierarchy. Someone is giving you the allowance. A parent gives a child an allowance for completing tasks. A judge gives an allowance on a ruling.

In order to receive the full value of an allowance, it is important that you feel worthy of receiving it. Both the giving and receiving of an allowance are based on trust. Trust is based on value and self-worth. As a child receives an allowance as an expression of trust from a parent, you can receive an allowance right now through trust in your higher self. Over time, the allowances you give yourself change the way you live. The richness of who you are on the inside begins to reflect on the outside.

Allowance can be a rite of passage for you now, just like it may have been as a child.

It is a big world out there—treat yourself to something new.

You deserve it!

ALLOWANCE CAN BE A RITE OF PASSAGE FOR YOU.

•   •   •

What is the relationship between receiving a childhood allowance from your parents, and you giving yourself an allowance as an adult?

I remember getting my first weekly allowance of fifty cents as a child for making my bed. Wow! What a sense of accomplishment! What a feeling of maturity! I couldn't wait for payday! I couldn't wait to buy more baseball cards!

As a teenager, I received a greater weekly allowance, which I didn't feel grew commensurately with the added chores I had to perform—such as taking out the garbage and mowing the lawn. I still enjoyed receiving the money, yet I had significantly less gratitude. My allowance had become a form of entitlement.

As an adult, between work and the kids, I was too driven and responsible to give myself much of an allowance. I did give myself one weekly allowance, however—playing in a Sunday softball league. This was a gift to myself that I treasured.

No sympathy necessary. After all, I was living my professional dream. Not only was I managing money in the stock market, I owned an investment firm that bore my name. However, with the onset of my partner's cancer, I began to experience emotional and mental pain deeper than anything I had ever felt. My powerlessness to heal her translated to increased sensitivity when the market went against me.

The stress and anguish led me deeper into my will to know and feel true security, beyond money. First, I gave myself a rather strange allowance—to the extent that an allowance often feels like a reward. I gave myself the allowance to realize my deepest fear: the fear of pain.

I had expended so much energy to avoid pain. I was the warrior wearing a coat of armor, slaying financial dragons by day, taking care of my son by night. Paying the bills. Keeping it together. It got to the point where I felt like Sisyphus, doomed to push a boulder uphill each day only to find myself at the base of the mountain each morning. I let go of the boulder...in trust.

I trusted something greater than pain. I took ownership of the belief that love of self and life exceeds pain. I knew without question that this belief had value beyond measure. I allowed myself to feel pain unlike anything I had ever felt. I was flooded with feelings of grief, rage and betrayal all at once. I was beyond tears, beyond breath, in one tight fetal cramp. There was only blackness.

In the midst of this agony, in the place I had avoided so desperately for so long, I asked for more pain. And more blackness.

After some period of time elapsed, the intensity of my pain began to subside. Pinholes of white light shone through the blackness. My essence, love, was breaking through. Every subsequent journey into pain resulted in more light and more of my essence shining through, until the whole fabric of the blackness shredded into oblivion. This allowance was most definitely a rite of passage for me.

I also gave myself a simple allowance to take walks in nature every day that it was possible. Being in nature helped me get in touch with my own true nature. I gave myself an allowance to speak my truth in both my personal and professional life. Each action step of my allowance changed the course of my life. I gave myself rewards, just like my parents did, for acts of self-sufficiency. Instead of cleaning my room, I was clearing the room for more spirit and life to flow through me.

This feels really liberating…to know that we can stop punishing ourselves and receive an allowance again. We finally have permission to live the life of our dreams!

What do you allow in your life?

What don't you allow in your life?

What can you allow in your life that you have not yet experienced?

What is your daily allowance?

What is your weekly allowance?

What is your monthly allowance?

Investment

Invest your money with your heart

and over time it will return with love.

Investment

Spring had fully blossomed at the ranch; the days were getting longer. The achiever was envisioning his new life. The visionary was now becoming achievement-oriented about the book they were writing. Together, they walked the land and talked about their message.

As they came to the end of the property, they sat by an oak tree. The achiever saw a vision of an enlightened economy—where people began to trust each other, and money was an expression of love. The visionary put his bare feet into the refreshingly cool creek and revealed his enthusiasm for a time when investors put their money where their heart is.

What are your investments?

Whereas allowance is a short-term expression of trust ...

Investment is a longer-term commitment.

Your financial investments are based on trust.

Your career is an investment based on trust.

Your marriage is an investment based on trust.

You invest your time.

You invest your money.

You invest your life energy.

Every investment you make involves inherent risk of loss.

Stocks can plunge.

Layoffs can occur.

Divorce can happen.

Every investment you make or evaluate has a risk/reward profile. Typically, the relationship of risk to reward is as follows: the greater the risk inherent in an investment, the greater the potential reward. Putting money in a savings account in a bank involves little risk and a low potential rate of return. Investing in a high technology company may entail a high risk and high potential return.

The goal of every investor is to identify and invest in those opportunities that offer the greatest return with the least risk. When you invest in what you want and love, your potential return is immeasurable—you are investing in your dreams. Your risk of loss may be minimal because there are so many ways for you to profit. Not the least of which is personal growth.

Are your investments congruent with what you want and love?

Are your investments aligned with your will?

WHEN YOU INVEST IN WHAT YOU WANT AND LOVE, YOUR POTENTIAL RETURN IS IMMEASURABLE—YOU ARE COMMITTING TO YOUR DREAMS.

I understand why you are asking these questions, but how can I apply this philosophy directly to my financial investments?

When you invest in a mutual fund, you are investing directly in the companies selected for you on your behalf. Do you know what the investment criteria are for stock selection? Is the investment philosophy of the fund manager consistent with your ideals and values? Do you trust that the companies they have chosen promote these ideals?

Conventional financial planning is based on numbers. It is recommended that you invest a certain percentage of your money in stocks, bonds and other investment vehicles, depending on your age and financial wealth. You can go beyond quantitative analysis, into a qualitative analysis. You can invest directly in companies and mutual funds that share your values and provide goods and services that you love.

Are you talking about socially responsible investing?

This extends far beyond the concept of socially responsible investing. Call this *personally responsible investing.* It is one thing to invest in companies that 'do no harm'; it is another to invest in companies and people that are proactively building the world in which you want to live. Personally Responsible Investing embraces your quest for personal sovereignty, the state of being in which you know that all your needs will be met from the inside out. Your Personally Responsible Investments are action steps with your time, energy and money that move you closer to living your dreams. If you manage your investment portfolio with this approach, you can experience success in addition to material gain.

PERSONALLY RESPONSIBLE INVESTING
IS PUTTING YOUR MONEY
WHERE YOUR HEART IS.

Successful investors invest in people and products they trust. They start by trusting themselves in their ability to analyze and make a competent financial decision. You can, too! Establish trust in yourself. Invest in that!

You are free to invest your resources into the areas that give you the greatest rate of return. You can manage your life as a series of investment actions in which each risk/reward relationship is in your favor.

Where can you get a return greater with less risk than an investment in yourself?

Your career is your investment. You literally spend almost half of your life working or parenting. For some, more than half your life; and for others—work is life! You alone are responsible for the job you have, because you have the free will to be there.

Does your work promote your inner security?

Go back to your will. Remember the dreams you had as a child. Maybe you wanted to be an astronaut. This may have been a burning desire. Did you revise your will and discover another career path for which you had even more passion? Or did you succumb to the inherited belief that you did not have the *right stuff?* The inherited belief that money equals security is often the deciding factor in the career path people choose.

If you have invested many years of your life in a career or job that no longer fulfills you, you can make a change. You are not alone. Every day, people revise their will and trust enough in themselves to take the leap of faith in a career change. This requires courage and self-love. You are always free to love yourself. Self-love has a value you can trust beyond compare. Courage is feeling your doubts or fears, and taking the desired action nonetheless. The greater your trust, the more energy and time you have to invest.

How can I apply this philosophy beyond career and money?

This holds true for the investment in your relationships as well. The more trust you have in yourself, the more you can trust somebody else. The more trust you have in your partner, the more you are willing to commit to the relationship. As you most likely know, love relationships can be challenging. Your will and the will of your partner are subject to revision in the course of your relationship.

For example, you may discover that your spirituality is paramount in your life now. In the past, it may have been completely unimportant to you. Your partner may not share your new sense of spiritual focus, despite your desire to share it with them.

View your investment in your relationship through the lens of personally responsible investing. Does your investment in this relationship support your true heart's desires? Can you invest in both your spiritual development and your relationship without compromising your true nature? Perhaps you need to invest some time alone in your spiritual practice, so that the relationship does not feel deficient. It is also possible that your new self-identity requires that the nature of your partnership evolve as you have.

So you are talking about investing in your values?

One of the lower risk forms of financial investing is called 'value investing.' A value investor invests in businesses that have minimal downside risk because of the worth of its underlying assets. With inner security, you are a value investor when you invest in your own values. As you trust and invest in your values, infinite wealth emerges from within you and materializes into your outer life in many forms.

One basic principle of investing is diversification. This means that you spread out your risk of investments by owning a variety of different kinds of investment. Diversification extends beyond financial investments. You can channel your life energies into multiple areas that promote your growth and your dreams. You can invest in your physical health, emotional well-being and spiritual development.

Through diversification you promote the virtue of balance in your life.

You can expand your bandwidth to become a new millennium renaissance person. There are a myriad of possibilities available if you allow yourself to reach out and discover...

You are not bound by the past.

This moment has never existed before!

Anything is possible!

THROUGH DIVERSIFICATION YOU PROMOTE THE VIRTUE OF BALANCE IN YOUR LIFE

Invest in yourself, in the people you love and in this very planet that is your home. You can invest in creating your vision of paradise on Earth.

Right now!

You can be the lead investor!

When you invest in what you love, your body becomes a temple, your home becomes a castle and the world becomes a paradise.

What does Heaven on Earth look like to you? What does it feel like? Let your imagination and desires run freely. Trust that your ideals do have priceless value and the power to actualize your visions. Diversify your investments into many areas that promote peace, health, personal sovereignty and sustainability. You can create a strategy to fulfill your dreams.

A strategic investor goes beyond putting money to work. Many venture capitalists are strategic investors, in that they invest their time and energy in conjunction with their money to ensure the success of their investment. They may be instrumental in attracting key personnel and even generating revenues through their established networks. You can enhance the probability of success as an investor when you treat your investments as strategic to your life goals.

•   •   •

How has this investment philosophy worked in your own life?

I invested in myself when I started my own business. I was making a lot of money in my position as a junior partner at a successful money management firm. My boss was very talented and completely focused on making money. However, I often experienced him as disrespectful, demanding and judgmental. I did my best not to take him personally, and told myself that it just came with the position. In reality, I sought out a voice in the outside world that mirrored my own self-critic.

So I frequently questioned my own sense of self-worth as a result of his judgments. I became so agitated at times, my will to continue to work at this firm began to diminish. My self-worth plummeted even as my net worth continued to rise. After a few months of inner conflict and soul searching, I got my will in order. It became clear to me that my deepest desire was to enjoy my career and enjoy my life again. I also had the lifelong dream of being my own boss.

To achieve my new dreams, I had to take ownership of the new belief that my happiness was more important than money. Even though I expected to earn significantly less money, it was more important for me to take this leap of faith in myself. Out of this trust, I made an investment in myself by investing a large portion of my net worth in the fund I was managing. This investment in myself attracted others to invest in me as well. I was living my dream.

During my tenure being my own boss, I gave myself an allowance to pursue my spiritual development in the context of my partner's cancer. As these experiences opened my heart and mind to the broader possibilities for my own existence, I took ownership of these actions, which I treasured and trusted whole-heartedly. I went back to my will and realized without doubt that my deepest desires changed again. I now desire to embody joy to its fullest and share it with others. Fueled by my will and funded with trust, I am a Personally Responsible Investor in my home, my family and my new business.

WHEN YOU INVEST IN WHAT YOU LOVE, YOUR BODY BECOMES A TEMPLE, YOUR HOME BECOMES A CASTLE AND THE WORLD BECOMES A PARADISE.

With an enormous personal trust account, each of us can give ourselves more than a regular allowance—we have abundant resources with which to invest directly and consciously in our values. Imagine a world in which each of us invested in areas that are founded on love and wholeness. It is possible!

How do you invest your time,
energy and money
in what you love?

Are your investments congruent with your values… and strategic to your life goals?

**How can you invest more in
yourself, the people
you love and the world you love?**

Appreciation

Appreciation is the greatest gift

you can give yourself and others.

Appreciation

What a life!

Sitting by the pool drinking fresh squeezed lemonade, watching the hawks circling the mountain valley. The visionary was grateful that he did not need to focus on the future—because he had the moment. He thanked his partner for giving him a chance to share a vision, and for his unconditional friendship and support.

The achiever expressed his gratitude to his visionary partner for suggesting a direction in which he could channel his love and creative energy. He expressed his gratitude to the visionary for inviting him to make a greater impact in the world and for helping him to experience greater meaning in his life. Together they appreciated the perfection of the moment in all of its simplicity and depth.

What do you appreciate?

Appreciation is an increase in value of your investment.

A stock appreciates in value.

Your house appreciates in value.

Even your baseball card collection can appreciate in value.

You can appreciate in value, too.

Your self-worth can skyrocket...

when you appreciate yourself—

when you give yourself an allowance—

when you invest in yourself—

when you trust in yourself.

When you appreciate all of the abundance in your life...

your abundance appreciates.

You are becoming your biggest cheerleader as opposed to your biggest critic. You are taking the action steps necessary to change the course of your life consciously and willfully. You are actively supporting your deepest desires. Because you trust that your actions are based in love, you move more confidently with fewer self-judgments.

As you encounter less and less resistance within and around you, you can experience a greater sense of grace and flow. The struggles of the past are just that—of the past. They no longer exist.

That is something you can appreciate!

Appreciation can occur over time—and it starts right now. As you give yourself an allowance, you appreciate yourself in the short term. For instance, giving yourself an allowance of a weekly massage is something that your body can appreciate. In addition to bringing pleasure and healing to your body, you are also clearing your mind of the stress associated with the past and future. You are allowing yourself to appreciate the moment.

If I invest in what I love, how can I promote greater love in my life through my investments?

When you invest in yourself, the people, products and services you love, you appreciate yourself over a long-term horizon. For example, you can invest in solar energy for your home or business. You may love investing in a renewable energy source that does not pollute the environment. You may love watching your electricity meter spin backwards as you sell your power back to your utilities company. You may love reducing or even eliminating your monthly electricity bill. You may love being independent from rolling power outages. You may love your new relationship with the sun—not only does the sun sustain all life on the Earth, but now it also powers your lights and toaster.

The financial return on your solar investment may take several years for payback. However, you can be appreciating your investment in solar power this very moment. Right now, you can appreciate your contribution to a clean and healthy environment. You appreciate your actions that support your values.

In appreciating your values, you increase your self-worth. That is something in which you can trust even more. Funded with this greater trust, you have even greater resources from which to give yourself an allowance or make an investment. This is how you compound your personal growth into infinite wealth and the life of your dreams.

Through appreciation, you experience inner security.

You appreciate the miracle of your very existence.

You appreciate feeling love without limits.

You appreciate the power of your free will.

You can even appreciate all of the pain and struggle you have ever directly experienced. All of these feelings and events in your life have led you to this moment.

BY APPRECIATING YOURSELF, YOU INCREASE YOUR SELF-WORTH.

What do you say to all of the people that don't appreciate their struggles in life?

There *are* moments when we do not feel appreciation for past adversity, or even for ourselves in the present. In these moments, you are either living in the past or the future. You may be stuck in a moment that has passed, dwelling on regrets, resentments or self-judgments. This prevents you from appreciating this moment.

If you are worrying about the future it is important to remember that...

This moment has never existed before.

Anything is possible!

When worrying about the future, you miss the opportunity to appreciate what you have in this moment. If you are stuck in the past or the future, you are caught up in inherited beliefs that prevent you from realizing your dreams.

One form of fear about the future is greed. Greed is borne out of inherited beliefs of scarcity. When a person is in a state of greed, they do not appreciate what they have in this moment and who they are in this moment. There is never enough. For them, something is truly missing that money cannot buy.

Sense if you have any traces of greed inside of you. How does it feel in your body? Does it feel powerful? Or not? Do you feel closer to your Creator? Do you feel this is who you really are? Do you feel this is who you want to be?

Through greed, your possessions may wind up owning you. Greed is the process of devaluing your self-worth into dollar terms. Greed is a form of devaluation, and that is how money became de-based.

Greed requires struggle. Instead of enjoying what you have now, you are expending your time and energy on making more money, no matter what the cost.

What is the price of greed? What does it cost you? Does it cost your integrity? Does it cost you honesty? Does it cost love with others?

Greed is a form of addiction. A greedy person can be addicted to money, love or attention. Greed is insatiable. There is a distinction between a feeling of insatiability and a sense of limitlessness. Insatiability is like a bottomless pit that can never be filled. It is a state of perpetual lack. There is neither contentment nor fulfillment.

Who wants that?

Why not count your blessings with gratitude instead?

WHEN WORRYING ABOUT THE FUTURE, YOU MISS THE OPPORTUNITY TO APPRECIATE WHAT YOU HAVE IN THIS MOMENT.

Gratitude is a heartfelt expression of appreciation. It is difficult to experience what you want without appreciating what you have. Gratitude opens the space to allow the miracle and the abundance of life to flow to you.

In this moment, in this breath, choose to feel the blessing of your life. Feel how deeply you can love. Appreciate that right now. Be content right now, even if you have not yet fulfilled your deepest heart's desires.

When you appreciate yourself, you begin to appreciate others. You enjoy expressing your gratitude and spreading good cheer. Appreciation is contagious. As you appreciate others, you will discover more people appreciating you.

In a business setting, this can be a true asset. One of the greatest expenses a company faces is client turnover. An organizational culture that embodies gratitude in customer relations will increase profitability.

Appreciation is a foundation for exchange between yourself and the world in which you live. It opens the door to more meaningful interactions and a sustainable way of life.

AS YOU APPRECIATE OTHERS, YOU WILL DISCOVER MORE PEOPLE APPRECIATING YOU.

. . .

Appreciation seems to be such an important factor in the service industries. I really enjoy spending my money when I hear the people serving me genuinely expressing their appreciation for my business. How has appreciation impacted your work in the business world?

A significant element of growth in my own money management firm occurred through appreciation. I appreciated a limited partner who was more than a financial investor— he was a strategic partner. We came to an agreement in which he referred me to other potential investors. I agreed to pay him a percentage of any income I would make on any of his referrals that I was able to convert into an investor.

Through his referrals and recommendations, I was able to grow my business significantly. As my fund performed well, the investors he referred began to refer other potential investors to me. My agreement with this strategic partner did not address this second-generation referral. I knew in my heart that I would not be receiving any of these new referrals if it had not been for my strategic partner and his direct set of referrals to me. Without negotiation or hesitation, I told my strategic partner that I was going to pay him the same percentage on all second-generation referrals, as if he had directly referred them himself.

I appreciated my strategic partner. He appreciated me by substantially increasing the money amount of his investment without any expectations from me. This is how appreciation increases flow, attracts greater appreciation, and even greater flow. This applies to my self-appreciation and self-worth as well.

I have made significant investments in myself, such as liquidating my money management firm, buying a twenty-acre ranch and writing this book. I appreciate every step along the path that has led me to this moment.

I appreciate with deep gratitude my renewed sense of self-worth. I do so with humility, because I appreciate all the moments of doubt, pain and fear that I have ever experienced.

I appreciate my former boss because he contributed significantly to my personal and professional development, my moments of discomfort notwithstanding. These experiences were essential life lessons that contribute to the awareness I have now.

WITH GRATITUDE, YOU ALLOW THE MIRACLES OF LIFE TO FLOW TO YOU.

I Appreciate

I appreciate being an American.

I appreciate my heart because I can feel so deeply.

I appreciate my will because I am completely free to dream and desire.

I appreciate my inheritance for all of its strengths and weaknesses.

I appreciate my ability to claim a self-identity that is aligned with my heart's desires.

I appreciate my values because they give my life more meaning and richness.

I appreciate my trust—in God, in myself and in others.

I appreciate the allowance I give myself that brings me closer to living my dreams.

I appreciate my investments in myself, in the people I love, in the products and services I love and in this planet that I love.

I appreciate the miracle of my existence.

• • •

Just as money can appreciate over time, so can life. What I didn't appreciate years ago, I can now.

How do you appreciate yourself?

How can you appreciate
yourself even further?

How can gratitude raise the quality of your life experience?

**Do you appreciate your life
and all that you have...
right now?**

Exchange

You have the ability to exchange money

as an expression of love.

Exchange

Labor Day—The sun was shining brightly. The delivery of the message contained in these pages was rapidly approaching. The visionary and the achiever reflected to each other how they were experiencing deeper levels of inner security and infinite wealth.

Now it was time for them to share their enthusiasm and vision in the world of exchange, a world currently dominated by fear. They both realized that, as messengers, they were prepared to walk their talk and talk the walk.

What do you exchange?

You exchange every day.

Exchange glances.

Exchange telephone numbers or business cards.

Exchange stocks.

Exchange money for goods and services.

Exchange time and energy for pay.

Exchange words.

Exchange vows.

Exchange expressions of love.

Exchange is an act of giving and receiving. Through exchange, you interact with the world around you. When you give a heart-felt smile to someone, even to a total stranger, you are more likely to receive one. When you interact with anger or rage, you are likely to encounter resistance in the form of defensiveness or anger in return. The content and impact of your exchanges depend on your inner feelings and beliefs.

Once again, the inner creates the outer. Inner security is a state of *being*. Exchange is a state of *doing*. Exchange activates your inner security into the outer world.

Each element of inner security takes on greater dimension and grows through exchange.

Where does it begin?

It starts with your will.

When you want something you love, you begin a process of drawing it to you through your will. For instance, let's say you really love the look and feel of a 1965 Mustang. Through your will, you set the intent to materialize it into your life. This may require revising your will, by exchanging the priorities you have for your money, so that buying the Mustang is at the top of your list.

EXCHANGE BASED IN INNER SECURITY SPREADS GREATER TRUST AND COMPASSION INTO THE WORLD.

You may be limited by inherited beliefs. Your father may have taught you to never buy a used car because you can never trust who is selling it to you. If you do not get past this belief, you will not manifest this dream. You must exchange this limited belief for another belief, such as—there are honest people in the world who want to sell a 1965 Mustang to you. Your love for the car is so great that you are willing to exchange the limited beliefs of your father for another perspective that supports your dreams. Perhaps there is someone out there with this car for sale that loves the car as much as you do.

Remember, anything is possible!

Take ownership of the qualities of discernment, diligence and patience that may be required for your car quest to become realized. You alone are taking responsibility for gathering all of the data necessary on which to base your decision. This may include mechanical inspections and investigating the reputation of the seller.

Before you purchase the car, assess its market value as well as its value to you personally. Review your basic values, such as standards for safety and environmental considerations. Once you have determined that it is in alignment with your values, trust your ability to make a competent decision. Trust that your actions are based in love—love for the car and love for yourself.

You are now ready to give yourself an allowance to buy the car, and permission to enjoy it. You are investing all of your resources—your money, time and energy—into an area of your life based in love.

Each time you sit behind the wheel of your 1965 Mustang, you can appreciate the car and, more importantly, yourself. Appreciate the seller for providing you with the opportunity to fulfill this dream. Appreciate the money you are exchanging in return for this car. You are offering the seller an opportunity to exchange this money for something they want and love as much as you love that Mustang.

Exchange born out of inner security spreads greater trust and compassion into the world. Centered in your inner security, you create greater ease and flow in your life and the lives of those with whom you exchange.

In a state of inner security, you are at peace. You have a strong and ever-growing sense of self-love and self-worth. You are free, free as your will, to feel and to love as completely as you are able in the moment. You have trust and faith that this moment is perfect, even with its seeming imperfections. You know you are no longer bound by the past. Your trust and faith are so great that you are free from worry about the future. Your exchanges have already begun to take on greater meaning to you as your actions have initiated your desired transformation.

You have exchanged certain inherited thoughts and beliefs that do not serve you. In return, you have received and claimed ownership of other perspectives and virtues that do provide a solid foundation from which your dreams can be actualized. You have claimed ownership of your life and your self-identity. You are cultivating your own field of dreams!

WITH INNER SECURITY, YOUR EXCHANGES BECOME MORE VALUABLE TO YOU AND OTHERS.

In order for many of our dreams to become manifest, we need money. Where does money fit in?

Money is the fertilizer with which some of these dreams can grow into full bloom. If you don't spread it around, you limit its growth.

Money is the medium of exchange in this world.

Imagine that you were alive at a time when money was originated. There you were in your tribal culture. You had the basics of food, clothing and shelter down pretty well, at least by primitive standards. People have begun to exchange in the form of barter, trading food for clothing and other essentials. Since your most basic needs are being met and you have learned to meet them more effectively than before, you have discretionary time in which to dream and create.

With discretionary time, you begin to desire and invent discretionary items. At first, these products help you to meet your needs even more efficiently. Baskets, pottery and flint arrowheads are examples of this first wave of technology that make your life easier. With the availability of more goods, barter reaches its limits.

You say to the basket weaver, "Mr. Weaver, I love your basket. I would love to own it, to use it to store my foods, to enjoy its patterns and colors."

The weaver replies, "Thank you for your loving, kind words. However, you have nothing I love as much as you love my basket."

You respond, "I understand. Here, let me give you these ten stones in exchange for your basket. These stones are beautiful, precious and very rare. Then, Mr. Weaver, you can take these stones and exchange them with someone else for something you love as much as I love your basket."

Cha-ching! We have an exchange using money in the form of stones.

At its core, this exchange is love. A basket that is loved is exchanged for stones, which are to be exchanged for another object of love. Money is the conduit, the currency through which the loving energy is transmitted. The conduit consists of trust.

Money only works if it is accepted as the medium of exchange, and it is only accepted if the receiver trusts that they can exchange the money for something else of equal value.

Imagine that money really did begin as an expression of love. Yet, in today's modern culture, money is rarely perceived as a demonstration of love. Did money *fall from grace* when it was exchanged without appreciation? Was money once a pure form of direct heartfelt appreciation and trust?

If it was, then over time it became a devalued currency for impersonal exchange. From the impersonal vantage point, money could readily be used to impose will, instill fear and abuse power.

To prevent money from losing all meaning, standards were set to instill trust. For thousands of years, gold has been a standard for money because of its brilliance, purity and scarcity. Clearly, basing financial wealth on a scarce commodity inherently limits its opportunity for growth. That is the primary reason why the gold standard was abandoned in the United States.

So, if your money was once worth its weight in gold, what is the standard on which it is based today?

The answer is—your standard.

Ultimately, you choose the criteria on which your money is based.

What are your standards?

As you consider the answer to this question, remember what you value most, what you appreciate most, what you trust most and what you want and love most.

The purity of money as an expression of love based on trust is our inheritance and our creation.

We can choose now, in this moment, to reclaim this inheritance.

We can choose now to raise our money to a higher standard.

We can choose now to use our money once again as our ancestors may have—as a currency of loving energy.

It sounds like a paradox to talk about using money as a currency of love, when money is being used with such

destructive intent. How does each one of us demonstrate the principle that money is an expression of love?

THE PURITY OF MONEY AS AN EXPRESSION OF LOVE BASED ON TRUST IS OUR INHERITANCE AND OUR CREATION.

One simple way is by loving what you do with your money. You can love attending the theater, traveling the world, buying a used car or even a piece of chocolate. You can feel a deep sense of gratitude for the joy and comforts money offers you. You can convey your gratitude along with your money in all your exchanges so that your money has greater meaning to its receiver. This is another form of appreciation wherein your money takes on even more value.

When what you do with your money creates love, you are raising money to the highest standard. Redirect your money based on this new awareness. Change your spending patterns towards goods and services that improve your personal well-being and that of your home, Earth.

In fact, this isn't even spending.

It is Personally Responsible Investing—

in yourself, your loved ones, your planet...

with an unlimited potential return:

for appreciation—

For paradise.

The essences of money and love are the same. Money growth is dependent on velocity. Velocity is the frequency of the exchange—the faster money changes hands, the greater its growth rate. If money sits in a mattress without exchange, it does not grow.

WHEN WHAT YOU DO WITH YOUR MONEY PROMOTES LOVE, YOU ARE RAISING MONEY TO THE HIGHEST STANDARD.

Love works the same way. You can go off into a cave and be in a loving state, and you can possibly reach an exalted state of enlightenment off by yourself. However, your love can grow so much faster when it is exchanged with another. In that exchange, you now have the love of another inside you as well as your own love, so that you have even more love to exchange.

Moreover, the person with whom you have exchanged love now has your love inside of them in addition to their own love, so that they have even more love to exchange as well. As both of you share all of this added love with others in the world, others have more love to exchange also.

With inner security, you know how precious you are. You are a diamond. You are pure, clear and brilliant, with infinite facets. You illuminate others with your radiance. And you are illuminated by the love of others. Your romantic partner reflects your brilliance. Your children, parents, colleagues and friends all illuminate facets of your diamond.

As you have infinite facets, there are no limits to how brightly you can shine, how deeply you can love, how diverse your life experiences can be. There are no limits to your capacity for exchange. This is infinite wealth!

You can exchange who you have been for who you want to be.

You can exchange any beliefs that hold you back for others that promote your individual sovereignty.

You can exchange any dreams you may have outgrown for even greater ones.

There are no limits.

There certainly are enough people with great sums of money that could really change the evolution of this planet by using their money as an expression of love. How do you address them?

Those of you who are blessed with significant financial wealth today: you are the gatekeepers of tomorrow.

For what purpose do you believe you have been blessed with so much financial resource?

YOU CAN EXCHANGE WHO YOU HAVE BEEN FOR WHO YOU WANT TO BE.

What do you want to create with all the influence you have?

What do you want to create in terms of short-term allowances for yourself?

What leaps of investment for the long haul do you want to make yourself, for everyone you love?

What do you want to build with all the creative energy and expression you have?

What do you want the world to inherit from you in exchange for your receiving the miracle of your very existence?

What is your will?

You are free and have rights.

You have the absolute right to diversify beyond your past investments.

You have the absolute right to choose what you do want to create in your life, including investing in what you love.

You have the absolute right to live your life with love as the highest standard!

Our mutual dream of a world living in harmony can become a reality. Anything is possible! We can transform the world of commerce from one based on the belief of struggle and scarcity to one based on appreciation and abundance. If we are able to determine that in our lives love is the highest value, then why not carry it out into the world and determine that love can be the highest standard in business, education and politics.

Are you willing to exchange
struggle in your life…
for flow?

Are you willing to exchange
fear and greed…
for love and compassion?

Are you willing to exchange the
limitations of the past…
for the infinite possibilities
of this moment?

Can you exchange money as an
expression of love?

WILL YOU?

EPILOGUE: THE MERGER

The evening of September 10, 2002

It has been one year since the conception of this book.

Tomorrow marks the one-year anniversary of the destruction of the World Trade Center.

We are all connected through its ashes.

We have experienced firsthand that anything is possible.

It is possible that what we take for granted can crumble in an instant.

It is possible that through the fire in our bellies and passion in our hearts, we can rise like a phoenix from the ashes.

During the past year, we witnessed several multi-billion dollar corporations fall from grace and leave a path of ruin in their wake: the loss of people's jobs and their savings for the future. Additionally, these events stirred up the winds of mistrust: in our institutions, in our investments. The events of the past year still have most of us contemplating the true meaning of security.

With our burning desire for inner security and infinite wealth, we are the alchemists that can transform our lives into the purest form of wealth.

We are waking up to our dreams, as our outer reality no longer reflects who we are on the inside.

When our outer lives completely reflect our inner selves, the merger is consummated.

Imagine, one day, that every person in the world awakens to the inner security alive within them. Imagine, further, that all exchanges are then based on this inner security. We would all be living the merger. The merger between:

Inner and outer,

    Self-worth and net worth,

        Being and doing,

            Work and play,

                Money and love,

Heaven and Earth.

Heaven on Earth exists for each of us in every moment, if we choose to realize it.

Collectively, we have all the wisdom, creativity, resources and money we need.

With inner security, life is a blockbuster movie.

You are the star.

You are the director.

You are the screenwriter.

You are the hero.

This is your love story.

This is your incredible adventure.

This is the beginning.

THIS MOMENT HAS NEVER EXISTED BEFORE...
ANYTHING IS POSSIBLE!

HEAVEN ON EARTH EXISTS FOR
EACH OF US IN EVERY MOMENT
IF WE CHOOSE TO REALIZE IT.

INNERSECURITIES

Contact authors at:

Inner Securities, Inc.
4160 Suisun Valley Road
Suite E, #416
Suisun Valley, CA 94534-4018

Phone: (707) 425-2360
Fax: (707) 434-9416

Email: info@innersecurities.com

Please visit our website for information about workshops,
web-seminars and consulting services.

www.innersecurities.com

Do you want to further enrich your life with Inner Security and Infinite Wealth?

We hope you found *Inner Security and Infinite Wealth* to be of significant value to you in your daily life. We have created an organization, Inner Securities, Inc., dedicated to creating opportunities for you to deepen your experience of Inner Security and Infinite Wealth. We offer an array of innovative programs to assist you in cultivating greater inner security and a more fulfilling relationship to money and your self.

Inner Securities IS Mastery, our training and consulting division, offers individuals, groups and corporations a fresh approach to financial security and wealth beyond money.

Specialty programs include:

■ **The Inner Securities Exchange**
A series of engaging weekly tele-broadcasts addressing topics of personal and global security. Additionally, you will have exclusive access to our online Exchange board.

■ **Eight Treasures of Inner Security and Infinite Wealth**
Using the *Eight Treasures of Inner Security and Infinite Wealth*™, you will deepen your discovery of how each of the "Treasures" magnetizes your dreams into a living reality.

For more information about IS Mastery programs and other Inner Securities, Inc., products and services, as well as our complimentary monthly newsletter *The Monthly Allowance*, we invite you to our website: www.innersecurities.com or to call: (707) 425-2360.

Inner Securities, Inc.
4160 Suisun Valley Road, Suite E–416
Suisun Valley, CA 94534-4018
Phone: (707) 425-2360
Email: info@innersecurities.com